PHOENIX AND MARICOPA COUNTY, ARIZONA

by
Janet Lauster Witzeman
Salome Ross Demaree
Eleanor Leland Radke

PUBLISHED BY MARICOPA AUDUBON SOCIETY

1997

Proceeds from the sale of this publication go to support the Maricopa Audubon Society and the Hassayampa River Preserve.

Published by
Maricopa Audubon Society
P.O. Box 15451
Phoenix, AZ 85060

Second Edition

Library of Congress Catalog Card Number:
96-78089

ISBN 0-9654566-0-9

Produced by
Eldon Publishing

TABLE OF CONTENTS

INTRODUCTION

This is the second edition of a book published in 1972. At that time we stated that it was a preliminary list because there were still many areas of Maricopa County that had not been adequately covered. It was intended as a base to learn what gaps needed to be filled. And fill them we did! During the twenty-five years since that first publication when the Maricopa County List totaled 346 species, 89 species have been added to the County List, including 23 species of shore and water birds and 18 species of warblers.

The new total of 427 species, plus one hypothetical species, includes four species gained from taxonomic "splits" that have occurred since 1972 – Clark's Grebe, Cordilleran Flycatcher, Red-naped Sapsucker, and Red-breasted Sapsucker. Four species from the old list were lost when three species of flickers and three species of juncos were "lumped" by taxonomists into Northern Flicker and Dark-eyed Junco respectively. However, one of those, the Gilded Flicker, has been returned to full species status. The old list also included five species that have been deleted from the new list: Ring-necked Pheasant, White-winged Pheasant, Chukar, Ringed Turtle-Dove, and Nuttall's Woodpecker. Nesting records for 37 species have been added since the first edition, making a total of 171 nesting records for the county. Four species no longer nest in the county – Osprey, Ferruginous Pygmy-Owl, and Belted Kingfisher nested historically, and Sora was still nesting as recently as 1975.

Maricopa County, encompassing 9,266 square miles, is as large as the state of New Hampshire. With elevations ranging from under 700 feet to over 7000 feet, there is a great variety of habitat found – from the low elevation creosote flats up to the pines and Douglas firs of the higher elevations, and including both wet and dry areas.

Twelve first state records have come from Maricopa County and, of these, four (in boldface) represent the only state records: Yellow-billed Loon, White-tailed Tropicbird, Red-billed Tropicbird, Cattle Egret,

Roseate Spoonbill, **Tufted Duck**, White-tailed Kite, Ruddy Turnstone, **Ruff**, **Wandering Tattler**, **Sharp-tailed Sandpiper**, and Glaucous Gull.

Maricopa County is probably the easiest place in the U.S. to see Inca Dove, Verdin, Bendire's Thrasher, Le Conte's Thrasher, Gray Vireo, Abert's Towhee, and perhaps Greater Roadrunner. The problem with finding Roadrunners is that they know when you are looking for them and will stay hidden. However, when you are out for a day of birding and not thinking of them, you will see one. So our advice to visiting birders is to try not to think about them.

We dedicate this book to Bob Norton, who was the first to keep a Maricopa County List, the first to keep a county year list, and who inspired us to compile and publish the first list. He was an active birder in Maricopa County from 1965 until his recent retirement and move to the state of Washington. His many contributions to Maricopa County records include the first state record of Ruddy Turnstone in 1966.

Verdin
Marilyn Hoff Stewart

ABOUT THE AUTHORS

Janet Witzeman began birding as a child with a favorite aunt who took her on the Sunday morning birdwalks at Shaker Lakes in Cleveland, Ohio. Her interest in birds was later rekindled at those same Shaker Lakes by her birder husband-to-be. Since moving to Phoenix in 1958, she has served as Field Trip Chairman and Secretary for the Maricopa Audubon Society. She organized and was co-compiler of the Phoenix Christmas Counts for 12 years in the late sixties and seventies. Janet has been keeping records and writing the Field Observations column for *The Roadrunner* and *The Cactus Wrendition* for 27 years. During the seventies and eighties she was a Southwest Regional Editor for *American Birds* for 12 years. She was the publisher and co-editor of *Continental Birdlife*. A charter member of the American Birding Association, she has served on the board of directors of the ABA as well as Western Field Ornithologists. She has been secretary of the Arizona Bird Committee for 21 years.

Bix Demaree began birding as a child in Vermont with her father. She has participated in Christmas Bird Counts for over 50 years. She has been actively birding and keeping records since she and her husband moved to Phoenix in 1945. In 1953 she was one of the founders of the Maricopa Audubon Society. She was co-compiler of the Phoenix Christmas Counts for 25 years, and a leader of the weekly bird walks at Encanto Park and Papago Park for 30 years. Bix has served as President and Education Chairman for the Maricopa Audubon Sociey, and was a trustee of The Arizona Nature Conservancy for 9 years. She is one of our most active field trip leaders and has guided many visiting birders. She is a charter member of the American Birding Association. She has authored several articles including "Nest Building, Incubation Period, and Fledging of Black-chinned Hummingbird" in the *Wilson Bulletin* (1971) and "Observations on Roof Nesting Killdeer" in the *Condor* (1975).

Eleanor Radke's interest in birds began as a child growing up in

Wyoming. Her serious study developed when she and her husband moved to a rural area of upstate New York. She co-founded a bird club and a wildlife sanctuary in that area. At that time she applied for, and was granted, a bird-banding license. After moving to Cave Creek, Arizona in 1964, she continued banding, and served as the editor of *North American Bird Bander* for 20 years. Her chief study was raptors. Eleanor was editor of *The Roadrunner* (predecessor of *The Cactus Wrendition*) for several years. Presently she is a bird rehabilitation volunteer, is doing a study of bird behavior, and continues as an editor with Eldon Publishing.

Abert's Towhee
Marilyn Hoff Stewart

ACKNOWLEDGEMENTS

MAJOR CONTRIBUTORS

Pat Beall, who compiled the Birding Areas section, began birding as a child in her back yard in Massachusetts, and has been an avid birder in the county and state since 1976. She has served as Treasurer, Membership Chairman, and Education Chairman for the Maricopa Audubon Society, having given many bird slide programs to schools and organizations. She also taught a beginner birding class at Scottsdale Community College. She is one of our most active field trip leaders and a frequent guide for out-of-state birders.

Troy Corman has been actively birding in the county and state since 1980, when he moved to Phoenix from Pennsylvania. His observations have added a significant amount of data to the county records. In the late eighties, he spent three and a half years doing intensive studies on the birdlife of the San Pedro River for the Bureau of Land Management. He has worked for the Arizona Game and Fish Department since 1990, becoming the coordinator of Neotropical Migratory Birds and the Arizona Breeding Bird Atlas Project in 1992. He became a member of the Arizona Bird Committee in 1996. Troy reviewed all drafts of the text and charts, the accuracy of which were greatly enhanced by his additions and corrections. Many of the habitat designations were written by him. He reviewed and corrected versions of the Birding Areas, Birding Calendar, and Changes In Status of Species sections, provided data from other biologists, and answered innumerable questions.

David Stejskal began birding in Phoenix as a child, and has been one of the most active birders in the county and state since the age of 12 when he reported the first county record (then known) of Varied Thrush in a tree in his yard (as well as in that same tree – a Steller's Jay, a Western Scrub-Jay, a White-breasted Nuthatch, a Red-breasted Nuthatch, American Robins, and Cedar Waxwings – part of the big winter of 72/73 invasion of northern species). His many discoveries have added considerably to the knowledge of birdlife in the county during the past twenty years. He is a member of the Arizona Bird Committee, has served as a co-compiler for the Arizona seasonal reports in *American Birds* and *Audubon Field Notes* for eleven years, and is a professional bird tour leader for Field Guides Incorporated. David spent many hours reviewing the charts and text, filling in blanks, providing more accurate data for arrival and departure dates, expanding habitat designations, and defining more closely the status and abundance of species in each season.

Kenn Kaufman began birding as a child, has birded actively in Arizona since 1970, and in Maricopa County from the early seventies to the early eighties, when he added much new information to the county records. He served as co-compiler for the Arizona seasonal reports in *American Birds* for over five years, then as editor of all of the seasonal reports since 1984, and has been the associate editor of *American Birds* and *Audubon Field Notes* for eight years. He is a member of the Arizona Bird Committee and is on the Board of Directors of the American Birding Association. His book, *Advanced Birding,* his workshops, and many articles in bird journals and birding magazines, as well as his paintings and drawings, have added immeasurably to the knowledge of field identification and appreciation of birds. We are especially grateful to Kenn for his gift of the drawing of the Gray Vireo for our cover. He also reviewed drafts of the charts and text, made many additions and corrections, and provided much of the data for the *Empidonax* flycatchers. His review of the Introduction and History sections resulted in several welcome ideas and suggestions.

Tom Gatz has been birding and working with birds in the county and state as a biologist, first with the Bureau of Reclamation from 1981 to 1993, then with the U.S. Fish and Wildlife Service since 1993. In addition to compiling the Birding Calendar, he reviewed drafts of every section of the book, made many additions and corrections, and provided many useful suggestions and words of advice. He was the source of much of our data for White-tailed Kite and Bald Eagle. He brought data in the literature on Ferruginous Pygmy-Owl and Belted Kingfisher to our attention, and provided records from other biologists. He was also our chief proof-reader.

Bob Bradley has been birding in the county and the state since 1971. He has served as Field Trip Chairman for the Maricopa Audubon Society, and has been the co-compiler of the Phoenix and Salt/Verde Christmas Counts since 1979. He has conducted beginning birding classes for the Desert Botanical Garden and Rio Salado Community College, and has acted as a guide for a number of visiting birders. Bob reviewed drafts of the charts and text, as well as the Birding Areas section. He made many helpful additions and corrections.

The above contributors were also a constant source of encouragement and support, and the authors wish to express their gratitude for the time and effort they spent on behalf of this project.

ADDITIONAL CONTRIBUTORS

Some portions of the Birding Areas section were written by Charles Babbitt, Troy Corman, Dave Eshbaugh, Liz Hatcher, and Tom Hildebrandt. Others who helped scout areas and/or provided ideas, additions, and suggestions were Wade Beall, Scott Burge, Matt Chew, Steve Ganley, Roy Jones, Mark Larson, Helen Longstreth, Norm Shrout, Dick Todd, Anita Van Auken, and Bob Witzeman.

Rich Glinski, raptor biologist with the Arizona Game and Fish Department, provided information on Peregrine and Prairie Falcons, and reviewed the status of all of the raptors. Roy Johnson provided many records from the Johnson, Simpson, Werner Collection, as well as personal records from the Mazatzal Mountains for the first edition of this book. He also was one of the sources of information on Ferruginous Pygmy-Owl for this edition. Rob Marshall, from the U.S. Fish and Wildlife Service, provided historical data on Ferruginous Pygmy-Owl. (Data concerning the owls at Agua Caliente came from Gilman, 1909. Some Owls Along The Gila River in Arizona. *Condor* XI: 148. Information about the owls at New River came from Fisher, 1893. The Hawks and Owls of the United States In Their Relation to Agriculture. *U.S. Department of Agriculture Bulletin* No. 8: 199).

Gale Monson was the source of our information on American Dipper and Varied Bunting. Amadeo Rea provided his records of Black Vulture, Hammond's Flycatcher, Dusky Flycatcher, Le Conte's Thrasher, and Pyrrhuloxia for the first edition of this book. Historical information on Breninger and Gilman's study of Ferruginous Pygmy-Owl on the Gila River at the turn of the century, as well as information on the historical nesting of Belted Kingfisher on the Gila River, came from Amadeo Rea's book, *Once A River* (1983). Linwood Smith provided information on Black Vulture and the nesting of Prairie Falcon in the Sierra Estrella Mountains.

Dick Todd, the non-game biologist for birds and mammals for the Arizona Game and Fish Department from 1967 to 1987, discovered the first Clapper Rails in the county. His yearly censuses of these and other marsh birds provided most of the information in the charts, text, and History of the Changes In Species section on the status of Clapper Rail, Virginia Rail, Sora, and Yellow-headed Blackbird, as well as much information on herons and other waterbirds. Jim deVos, from the Arizona Game and Fish Department, provided information on the status of Wild Turkey.

Information on the Bald Eagle came from the coordinators of the Recovery Program: Larry Forbis of the U.S. Forest Service in the late seventies, Robert Mesta of the U.S. Fish and Wildlife Service in the eighties, and Greg Beatty of the Arizona Game and Fish Department in the nineties. Data on lowland records of Flammulated, Elf, and Saw-whet Owls came from Kathy Ingram, veterinarian at the Phoenix Zoo, and Megan Mosby from Liberty Wildlife Rehabilitation Foundation. Many historical records came from *Birds of Arizona* by Phillips, Marshall, and Monson (1964).

David Griffin provided data from the 1994-95 bird surveys in the Sauceda and Sand Tank Mountains, Barry M. Goldwater Air Force Range in southeastern Maricopa County. Roy Jones contributed records from the Phoenix Zoo. Steve Ganley compiled many records from the host of birders who contributed their observations. Gary Rosenberg, who has been an active birder and contributor to the county records since the late seventies, provided several useful ideas and suggestions.

We wish to thank Tom Gatz, Jill Jones, Roy Jones, Ken Rosenberg, Lloyd Shuttleworth, Dave Stejskal, Tom Stejskal, Dick Todd, and Bob Witzeman for the use of their photographs; and Brian Evans, Kenn Kaufman, Marilyn Stewart, and Larry Toschik for the use of their drawings.

Don Radke spent many extra hours preparing the charts and text for publication. Many thanks to Larry Manire at Techniprint for expediting the output.

We are indebted to Jak Keyser at Lithotech for donating so much of his time and expertise in preparing the maps, designing the covers, enhancing the photographs, and shepherding the whole book from raw data to finished product.

We thank Scott Burge for his generous donation toward the cost of making the maps.

Without the help of the above contributors and all of the observers who have contributed records over the years, this book would not have been possible. The authors wish to express their appreciation and thanks to all of them.

Bald Eagle nesting along Verde River
Brian Evans

ANNOTATED FIELD LIST **BIRDS**

of MARICOPA COUNTY, Arizona

Le Conte's Thrasher

Le Conte's Thrasher on cover of First Edition
Larry Toschik

HISTORY

OVERVIEW

From 1924 until about 1950, Ruth and Harry Crockett were virtually the only birders in Phoenix. We owe many of our early records to their meticulous observations and photographs. In July 1953, when the Maricopa Audubon Society was founded, there were still only a handful of birders in Phoenix. By the time the first Phoenix Christmas Count was conducted in December 1954, there were 51 members. At that time the population of Maricopa County was approximately 330,000. The first issue of the newsletter, *The Roadrunner,* was published in June 1954. The name was changed to *The Cactus Wrendition* in January 1984.

When the first edition of this book was published in 1972, there were about 650 members in the Maricopa Audubon Society, and the population of the county since 1954 had just about tripled to over 970,000. Another half million people were added during the seventies. Between 1980 and 1997 the population in the county grew by over one million people, with the result that we are now the nation's sixth most populous county with over 2.6 million. Phoenix has become the seventh largest city in the United States. Membership in the Maricopa Audubon Society has risen as well to over 2900. In short, we have lost habitat but gained many new birders.

The seventies saw a dramatic rise in birding activity in the county (as well as in the rest of the country) due in part to the population explosion of new, active, knowledgeable birders. One of those new birders, Scott Terrill, became the catalyst for change in Maricopa County when he moved here in 1973 and brought with him the California birding style of chasing rare birds, and birding small patches of trees and oases that came to be known as vagrant traps. His first call upon arriving here was to report the first county record of Red-eyed Vireo in the unlikely looking birding spot of the now famous Chandler Blvd. row of trees. Known then as Williams Field Road, it has since been responsible for providing many more rare county records. Under Scott's influence, birding went from casual weekly trips at well known spots to more frequent checks of smaller out-of-the-way places. One of his almost daily checks of areas on his way to classes resulted in the discovery of a Rufous-backed Robin in a small group of trees behind a store in downtown Tempe.

By 1974, inspired by Kenn Kaufman's 1973 record-breaking U.S. year list, nine of us decided to work on a county year list, and thought we would do well to reach a total of 240 species. But we underestimated the power of so many birders out in the field so often, especially during late summer and fall when nine scorching-hot trips were made to Painted Rock Dam, and the 35th Avenue Sewage Ponds received daily coverage. Scott Terrill ended the year with a total of 284 species and the rest of us were not far behind. The combined total number of species recorded in the county that year was 315. The intensity of that year's birding added twelve species to the county list, new arrival and departure dates, more accurate abundance status for many species, and exploration of hitherto rarely-birded areas in the county. By the time Scott left Arizona in 1981, the higher level of birding activity and birding expertise of all of the county's birders resulted in over 50 rare or accidental species having been added to the county list since 1972.

The seventies were also the best of times for the Phoenix Christmas Counts. The combination of excellent and varied habitats, favorable weather conditions, the active recruitment of the best birders in the state, and some from out-of-state, resulted in Phoenix having the highest inland counts in the U.S. in 1972 with 165 species, and in 1974 with 162 species. These high, over 150 species, counts continued through 1976. During the late seventies and early eighties the gradually declining habitat in southwest, west, and northwest Phoenix reduced the counts to 135 species and lower. This contributed to the decision to move the count in 1985 to its present location around the confluence of the Salt and Verde Rivers.

During the eighties and early nineties, numbers of birders and species of birds on the county list continued to grow. A rising interest in birding among residents and new birders moving into the county helped to add another thirty or so birds to the county list. Four projects initiated in recent years have made favorable contributions to the interest in birding in the county. In the mid-eighties, Lynn Vogel, Nancy Swanson, and Tillie Chew began conducting bird walks at the Desert Botanical Garden. These have evolved into weekly bird walks with the help of additional leaders Charlie Brenner, Joyce and Andy Buggs, Elizabeth Hubbell, Polly Schmidt, Andree Tarby, and Carolyn Wong. In 1988, Steve Ganley began producing the MAS Bird Alert – a weekly recorded message of bird sightings. People who had never participated in the birding network began to report interesting sightings about which we would not otherwise have learned. In 1990, Herb Fidel began teaching a Basic Birding class three times a year. Many of our most enthusiastic and active birders are graduates from these classes. In 1993, the Arizona Breeding Bird Atlas Project, coordinated by Troy Corman of the Arizona Game and Fish Department, was begun. This has been responsible for attracting many first time birders out into the field, and for producing new breeding data for the county and state.

CHANGES IN HABITAT

"Habitat, habitat, have to have a habitat." So goes the refrain from a song by environmental song writer Bill Oliver. Habitat for birds in Maricopa County has been declining since the early part of the century when dams built on the Salt, Verde, and Gila Rivers destroyed many miles of riparian areas. In recent years, an increase in the number of ponds and lakes in new housing developments has led to an increase in waterfowl species at the expense of species found in fields, hedgerows, and trees.

In the text are references to birding areas that no longer exist. Following is the history of some of those areas, as well as a discussion of some habitat we have gained.

Many birding areas that were productive in the fifties, sixties, and seventies have given way to housing or industrial developments. Unusual records came from places like the New River Ponds, Bennett's Marsh, Ramsey-Hazlett Farm and Pond, Tal Wi Wi Ranch, and Arrowhead Ranch in northwest Phoenix. In southwest Phoenix the old River Ranch at 43rd Avenue and the Salt River was a convenient place to see shorebirds and other migrants.

A favorite place to bird until the mid-eighties when it was sold, was the old Guernsey Ranch on the north side of the Salt River between 51st and 59th Avenues. The varied habitats there were a delight for birds and birders alike: tamarisks, mesquites, cottonwoods, elderberry bushes, fields, weeds, wood piles, and running water. Burrowing Owls had a small colony there, Bendire's Thrasher was often seen, and unusual migrants and wintering birds were frequently reported. It was there that the first Ruddy Ground-Doves were discovered. The final death knell sounded in 1988 when Broadway was extended and paved east of 59th Avenue through the ranch to 51st Avenue.

Probably the greatest loss was the 35th Avenue Sewage Ponds just north of the Salt River, which were drained and abandoned in the mid-eighties. Built in 1960, they were the best of both worlds, providing habitat for shorebirds as well as for waterbirds needing deeper water. Beginning at 23rd Avenue, a series of small ponds with mud flats led to the entrance of two large ponds, one-half mile across, that extended for a mile to 35th Avenue. Because of these ponds, there was an increase in shorebirds that formerly were considered rare in the county, such as Snowy Plover, Dunlin, Solitary Sandpiper, and Sanderling. Records new to the county from these ponds were Horned Grebe, Neotropic Cormorant, Black Scoter, Surf Scoter, White-winged Scoter, Wandering Tattler, Ruff, Red Phalarope, Long-tailed Jaeger, Heermann's Gull, Western Gull, and Sabine's Gull. Black-necked Stilts and American Avocets nested there, and Burrowing Owls nested between the ponds and the Salt River. The ponds also contributed greatly to the high numbers of species on the Phoenix Christmas Counts during the seventies.

The old Riggs Road Spreckles Sugar Ponds, east of McQueen Road in Chandler, built in 1972 and abandoned in 1982, provided many unusual shorebird records, most notably the first record of Sharp-tailed Sandpiper in the state. The old Avondale ponds, west of 123rd Avenue, were productive from 1982 to 1992. The Chandler Blvd. row of trees, where many unusual vireos, warblers, and finches were found, was cut down in September 1995.

On the plus side, we have the new Gilbert Wildlife Area Ponds which were enhanced by a Heritage Fund grant from the Arizona Game and Fish Department for a landscaping plan, as well as plantings done by volunteers. We also have the new wetlands project ponds at the 91st Avenue Wastewater Treatment Plant.

One of the biggest drawing cards for birds in the county is Painted Rock Dam. Since it was built in 1959, it has provided an inland sea above the dam during the flood years of 1966, 1974, 1978, 1979, 1980, and 1993. It has attracted such rarieties as Red-throated Loon, Yellow-billed Loon, Magnificent Frigatebird, Tricolored Heron, Reddish Egret, Wood Stork, Buff-breasted Sandpiper, Parasitic Jaeger, Laughing Gull, Glaucous Gull, Black-legged Kittiwake, Elegant Tern, Least Tern, and Black Skimmer. The area below the dam attracts shorebirds and other waterbirds, and provides nesting habitat for Western Grebes, Double-crested Cormorants, and three species of egrets.

CHANGES IN STATUS OF SPECIES

Horned Grebe was considered rare in the state in the sixties. The first to be documented in the county was in the fall of 1970. Since the mid-seventies, one or more individuals have been recorded each fall or winter in places like Fountain Hills, Gila Farms Pond, and Painted Rock Dam.

Western Grebe was not found nesting in the state until 1973 at Lake Havasu. In the county at that time, the species was present only from October through December, and from mid-April through May. By the mid-seventies there were several August, September, January, February, and March records. By the winter of 1978-79, many wintered below Painted Rock Dam and were observed giving their courtship dance there in March 1979. The group remained through the summer for the first time that year, but nesting was not confirmed until July 1980. From that time on, large numbers continued to winter below Painted Rock Dam, and a few remained through the summer. However, the second nesting was not recorded until the summer of 1991. Since then the species has been present year-round below Painted Rock Dam, and has nested there each summer since 1991.

Before the eighties, **Brown Pelican** was considered to be casual in late summer and fall when individuals would wander north into the county from July through September. By the early eighties, individuals began to remain into December, and to appear in spring at Painted Rock Dam, sometimes as early as March, then remain through the summer. By the early nineties, summer and fall numbers increased at Painted Rock Dam, sometimes to twenty at a time, and individuals began to spend the winter there.

Before the early seventies, **Double-crested Cormorant** was listed as a casual transient in the county. The first summer and winter observations were not recorded until 1974. Numbers in summer gradually increased below Painted Rock Dam until 1979 when the first nests were discovered there. Nesting was sporadic in the late eighties and early nineties, but since 1992, increasing numbers have nested there each year. Winter records in the Phoenix area have also increased in recent years.

There was only one county record for **Neotropic Cormorant** through 1970, an individual found at the 35th Avenue Sewage Ponds. The second record, and the first at Painted Rock Dam, was not until 1989. Since then, one or two have been present there off and on until December 1993. From that time to the present, one or more have been there continuously.

In 1930 a colony of nesting **Great Blue Herons** was found in cottonwood trees along the Salt River southwest of Phoenix at Avondale. After the death of those trees, no evidence of nesting was recorded in the county until 1972 when a colony was found in cottonwoods along the Verde River in the Fort McDowell Indian Community. Since then, nesting sites along the Verde River have increased on and north of Fort McDowell, as well as along the Salt River between Granite Reef Dam and the Verde River. Additional nesting sites were found below Painted Rock Dam in the early eighties, at Arlington in 1990, and along the Salt River southwest of Phoenix again in 1995.

Before 1972, there were no winter records and few summer records of **Great Egret** and **Snowy Egret** in the county. Along the Salt and Gila

Rivers southwest of Phoenix, both species were rarely recorded in winter until the early eighties. During the seventies and eighties, winter and summer records gradually increased below Painted Rock Dam. The first evidence of both species nesting in the county was below Painted Rock Dam in 1991. Since then nesting activity of both species has increased there each year.

The first record of **Cattle Egret** in the county and the state was in December 1966. From 1968 until 1972, only one or two individuals were seen each winter southwest and southeast of Phoenix. Numbers increased dramatically in December 1972 when 17 were counted in four areas of the Phoenix Christmas Count. By 1978, 88 were recorded on the Phoenix Christmas Count, and that winter high numbers were also recorded south of Chandler, in Tempe, Mesa, and Buckeye. In 1972 a few began to remain into May in the Phoenix area, and return as early as August. The first summer records at Painted Rock Dam were in July 1974. From that time on, small numbers were recorded each summer at Painted Rock Dam. In July 1990, young birds were reported with adults in southwest Phoenix. Nesting was suspected at Painted Rock Dam in 1992, and confirmed there in 1993. Nesting was suspected along the Gila River southwest of Phoenix in 1995.

During the sixties and early seventies, **Black-crowned Night-Heron** was listed as having bred formerly along the Salt and Verde Rivers. Immatures were reported with adults along the Salt River in southwest Phoenix in 1972 and below Painted Rock Dam in 1974. Nesting was confirmed along the Gila River, just west of the confluence with the Salt River, in the summer of 1974. In the late seventies and early eighties other nesting localities were reported at ponds in Scottsdale, at Arlington, and in areas east of Painted Rock Dam. The species began nesting in palm trees at the Phoenix Zoo in 1992.

Before the winter of 1974–75, there were no winter records of **White-faced Ibis** in the county. Eight individuals wintered at Painted Rock Dam that year. By the early eighties, individuals were reported at several locations around Phoenix in winter, and numbers at Painted Rock Dam continued to be seen each winter, with a high of 25 recorded there in January 1981. In the late eighties and early nineties, up to 20 individuals were reported each winter along the Salt River in southwest Phoenix. A high number of 80 were recorded on the Gila River Christmas Count in 1992.

Before 1970, **Black-bellied Whistling-Ducks** were seldom seen in the county. A pair was present at the old River Ranch during the summer of 1961. Two were reported at the 35th Avenue Sewage Ponds in the fall of 1963. Thirteen were counted at the old Union Hills Pond in northwest Phoenix in June 1968. A pair was reported in Peoria in June 1969. Throughout the seventies and early eighties, one or two (occasionally up to six or eight) were seen in spring, summer, and fall at the old Pima Road Pond in Scottsdale, the old Riggs Road Spreckles Ponds in Chandler, and the old 59th Avenue Pond on the Salt River in southwest Phoenix. The first winter record was of one that remained at the Youngtown Pond from October 1978 to March 1979 (and returned for two more consecutive winters). Numbers began to increase in the Chandler/Gilbert area in the early eighties, and a pair was found nesting at the Sun Lakes Ponds in 1984. The species has continued to nest there through the eighties until the present, as well as at the Gilbert Wildlife Area Ponds beginning in 1985, at the El Mirage Pond beginning in 1986, and at the old Avondale Pond in 1990 and 1991. Since 1990, fall and winter records have increased in Chandler from up to and over 100 at times, to 250 at one time.

The first record of **Ross' Goose** in the county was not until 1971. There were only three additional records in the seventies. It was not until the mid-eighties that the species became a regular winter visitor, and more than one individual was recorded each year.

The first **Eurasian Wigeon** in the county was photographed at Papago Park in 1966. The second was also recorded at Papago Park, but not until 1979. One has returned almost every winter since then to the Park or Zoo Ponds. By the mid-eighties, a second individual was recorded each winter elsewhere in the Phoenix area. Since 1990, up to four individuals have wintered each year in the Phoenix, Scottsdale, Mesa, Sun City, and Chandler areas.

The first **Greater Scaup** was not recorded in the county until 1974. Thereafter there were few records until the late eighties. Since 1989, from one to five individuals have been recorded each winter in the Phoenix, Peoria, Scottsdale, Mesa, and Chandler areas, as well as below Painted Rock Dam.

Although the first **White-tailed Kite** in the county was discovered at Blue Point along the Salt River in 1973, the next record was not until ten years later when one was observed at the Gila Bend Sewage Ponds. From that time until the present, numbers have increased each year, coinciding with the invasion that has taken place in the state since the early eighties. The species was first found nesting in the county in 1993 at Robbins Butte.

Bald Eagles have been nesting along the Salt and Verde Rivers east of Phoenix since at least the 1930s when there was at least one nest near Saguaro Lake and one near Bartlett Dam. In 1975, there were only three known nesting territories in the county and nine in the entire state. By 1995, the number of known breeding territories had increased to eight in the county and 36 in the state. The increase was due to a number of helping hands. In 1978 a Nest Watch Program was begun by the U.S. Forest Service with Audubon Society volunteers, then run by the U.S. Fish and Wildlife Service in the eighties, and the Arizona Game and Fish Department in the nineties. The Active Nest Search Project, begun in 1985, helped greatly in locating more territories. Both programs benefited from the cooperation received by the above agencies from the Bureau of Reclamation, Bureau of Land Management, Salt River Project, Southwest Bald Eagle Management Committee, and Native American Tribes.

Although there is an old record of a pair of **Harris' Hawks** that nested at the old Blue Point Cottonwoods on the Salt River from 1955 to 1971, there were few records in the county away from the Cave Creek/Carefree area before the eighties. Even there they were not common. In 1981, eight were counted in one day along the Verde River, and from then on there were increased sightings, including nesting, in Phoenix, Peoria, Tempe, and Scottsdale neighborhoods. Individuals have been observed along the Salt, Agua Fria, and Gila Rivers west of Phoenix, as far west as Paloma, and nesting as far east as Roosevelt Lake. They have become a common sight in Fountain Hills. Since 1985, the Salt/Verde Christmas Count has averaged over 100 individuals each year. A pair has been nesting at the Phoenix Zoo since about 1987.

In the early seventies, **Peregrine Falcon** was a rare winter visitor in the county. About 1973, numbers of wintering individuals began to increase. The first one to be noticed on top of one of the tall buildings in downtown Phoenix was in March 1977. By the early nineties there were half a dozen individuals each winter roosting and foraging from the tops of buildings in Phoenix and Mesa, feeding on pigeons and doves, and flying to sewage ponds for shorebirds and ducks. Since the mid eighties, the species has been found nesting on cliffs along the Salt River.

Before the first **Clapper Rail** was discovered in the county in June 1970 (a pair at 107th Avenue and the Salt River), the farthest east the species had been recorded in Arizona was at the Tacna Marsh on the Gila River east of Yuma. That same summer another individual was found below Granite Reef Dam. Since that time, other new sites were discovered in the county: a pair at Granite Reef Campground in 1975, a pair at 123rd Avenue and the Salt River in 1986, and one on the Salt River across from Coon Bluff in 1978, where the species (at least one pair) continued to nest until the mid-eighties. This marsh was the only one to survive the 1978 floods. Subsequent new sites were found at Arlington in 1982 when a high of 13 individuals (including three pairs) were counted, a pair east of Buckeye in 1985, and at least six east of Painted Rock Dam in 1988. The 1991 survey recorded a high of 50 Clapper Rails along the Gila River west of Phoenix from 115th Avenue to Citrus Valley, southwest of Gila Bend; over half of these were from Arlington. That same year two were detected at the place where they were originally recorded in the county. The 1994 survey recorded 55 Clapper Rails along the Gila River west of Phoenix, including a new area below Painted Rock Dam in Dendora Valley. The 1995 survey recorded 29 individuals, including a pair again in Dendora Valley. Two winter records may indicate that the species is present year-round, but overlooked because it is silent at that time of year. Clearly the success of this species in the county depends on the rise and fall of cattail marshes along the Salt and Gila Rivers after periodic spring floods that will continue to occur despite the dams.

The summer status of **Virginia Rail** in the county has always been that of a rare and local resident, dependent on cattail marshes. During the fifties the species was found nesting at the old Palo Verde Marsh (on the Gila River south of Palo Verde). Between 1978 and 1982, one or two pairs were found nesting at the marsh on the Salt River across from Coon Bluff. A new nesting site was discovered at Arlington in 1982. After 1983 there was no evidence of breeding there or anywhere in the county until May 1991 when the species was found at Blue Point on the Salt River, at two marshes near Buckeye on the Gila River, and on a tributary of the Agua Fria River, southeast of Avondale. In May 1994, a pair was found nesting at the confluence of the Gila and Agua Fria Rivers. In 1995, a pair was found nesting again at the marsh on the Salt River across from Coon Bluff.

Historical records indicate that **Sora** nested in the county in the fifties in marshes along the Salt River west of Phoenix, at Blue Point, and in Chandler. One was found at Blue Point in April 1973. In August 1974 an adult with one young was seen at the old Riggs Road Spreckles Ponds in Chandler, and in September 1974 an adult was seen with two young at the old Pima Road Pond in Scottsdale. Individuals were observed at a marsh on the Verde River in June 1975, and below old Lake Pleasant in August 1975. Although one individual was detected at the marsh across from Coon Bluff in May 1983, there has been no evidence of nesting in the county since the mid-seventies.

It is difficult to imagine that **Common Moorhen** was ever considered rare in the county. Although historical records indicate that ten were observed in a marsh near Tempe in 1933, that marsh was destroyed before 1940. The first record in "recent" times was of one that was discovered at a meat packing plant pond on McDowell Road, April 30, 1952. From that time on, numbers and sightings increased at such places as the old River Ranch, Tal Wi Wi, and at Bennett's Marsh where three juveniles were observed in June 1955. Numbers on the Phoenix Christmas Count increased from 17 in 1963 to 76 in 1968. By 1970 the species was considered to be a common resident, and was not as much of a skulker as it had been previously. In 1975, 235 were recorded on the Phoenix Christmas Count. Since the early eighties, the species has been a resident at the Phoenix Zoo, where it can be seen walking about, and even nesting, in the open.

From the early seventies to 1981, flocks of **Mountain Plovers** were regular winter visitors to fields near Painted Rock Dam and/or to fields in the Chandler area. Since then there have been only two records of single birds, and one record of four birds, in the county. They seem to have moved to fields farther south in Pinal County.

Black-necked Stilt was first found nesting in the county at the old 35th Avenue Sewage Ponds in 1963. By 1968 nesting also occurred at the 91st Avenue Sewage Ponds, in 1975 at the old Riggs Road Spreckles Ponds, and in 1978 at Painted Rock Dam. Some were present at Arlington in June 1982 and probably nested there. Nesting continued at ponds in southwest Phoenix through the eighties and early nineties, with additional sites along the Gila and lower Agua Fria Rivers during the nineties, at the old Avondale ponds in 1991, at the El Mirage Pond since 1991, and at the Gilbert Wildlife Area Ponds in 1994.

As of 1964 there were only three winter records of Black-necked Stilt in the state. One of these was of one in the county, west of Gila Bend, in February 1940. In 1968, ten were recorded wintering at the 35th Avenue Sewage Ponds. Winter numbers increased in southwest Phoenix and Avondale to as many as 63 in 1975, and up to 50 in the late seventies to the mid-nineties. By 1986, large numbers were found wintering at the Gilbert Wildlife Area Ponds. Since the early nineties, additional wintering areas have been at Sun Lakes (175 in 1992), Ocotillo, and other ponds in housing developments in Chandler.

American Avocet was first found nesting in the county at the 35th Avenue Sewage Ponds in 1969, and continued nesting there each summer through 1977. However, there was no evidence of breeding again until the summer of 1988 when at least eight pairs were found nesting in southwest Phoenix. About a dozen were observed acting territorial in Citrus Valley, southwest of Gila Bend, in May and June 1991, and may have bred there. In 1991 at least one pair nested at the Gilbert Wildlife Area Ponds, and by 1994 several pairs were found nesting there.

Since the early seventies, small numbers (and, rarely, higher numbers) have remained in southwest Phoenix, west of Phoenix, and recently at the Gilbert Wildlife Area Ponds almost every fall through December. There are only about five January records and two February records. For the first time, one individual spent the entire winter and into May 1992 at the Gilbert Wildlife Area Ponds.

California Gull is considered to be an uncommon transient and winter visitor in all of the county except for Painted Rock Dam. After the spring flood of 1993, large numbers moved into the large body of water there in July, and small numbers have remained and may take up year-round residence.

Like its cousin, the Inca Dove, that moved north into the state about 100 years ago, **Ruddy Ground-Dove** began a range extension into Arizona in the early eighties. The first record for the county and the state was of a pair discovered at the old Guernsey Ranch, October 21, 1981. The second record followed soon after with one seen at Rio Verde, December 31, 1981. There were only two more records, in 1984 and 1985, until 1989 when the range extension began to accelerate. From that time through the fall/winter of 1992-93 there were seven more records. The first spring record, and the first nesting record for the county and the state, was of a pair and fledgling discovered at the Hassayampa River Preserve, May 15, 1993. The second spring record, also May 1993, was of one at Rio Verde. There were five additional county records through the fall/winter of 1994-95.

At the close of the nineteenth century into the early 1900s, **Ferruginous Pygmy-Owl** was considered to be a common resident in cottonwoods at the confluence of the Salt and Gila Rivers, was found nesting in a palo verde tree at Agua Caliente at the western edge of the county, and found nesting in mesquite trees at New River. Until the fifties the species was still a sparse resident in the county, in the cottonwood and mesquite habitat near the confluence of the Salt and Verde Rivers. Except for an individual heard in 1971 at the historic Blue Point cotton-woods (burned in 1977), there have been no records of this species in the county since 1951.

Up until the early eighties, **Burrowing Owls** were commonly seen along the north side of the Salt River east of 35th Avenue, inside the 23rd and 35th Avenue Sewage Ponds, and just west of 51st Avenue at the entrance to the Guernsey Ranch, as well as at several other areas around Phoenix. By the mid-eighties, with dune buggies and dirt bikes having destroyed the habitat east of 35th Avenue, the demise of the 23rd and 35th Avenue Ponds, the eastern extension of Broadway Road from 59th Avenue through the Guernsey Ranch, and housing developments in former Burrowing Owl habitat, it became increasingly difficult to find Burrowing Owls in the county. Fortunately, they can still be seen at Scottsdale Community College, the Chandler Airport, and near Painted Rock Dam.

The first summer record and first breeding record of **White-throated Swift** in the county was in June 1973 when a group were observed nesting at Lake Pleasant. Some were observed flying over downtown Phoenix in June 1972, but it was not until May 1981 that several pairs were found nesting on the Arizona Bank Building in downtown Phoenix, and young were observed there in August. In May 1983 the species was found nesting on the Civic Plaza Building in downtown Phoenix, and on Camelback Mountain. It is suspected that they are nesting in cliffs along the Salt River and perhaps at Papago Park.

Anna's Hummingbird was first found nesting in the county in a Phoenix yard in November 1964. Soon after, a second nest was discovered in Sunnyslope in January 1965. The next evidence of breeding did not occur until February 1968 at Encanto Park. From December 1968 to March 1969, a female was observed successfully fledging young from three successive nests in one yard in Scottsdale. Nesting activity increased from that time on. However, there were still few summer records, as the species usually departed from the Phoenix area by early April and did not return until October. By 1971 a few returned in mid-September. In 1972, a female was still present in a Phoenix yard in mid-May, and one returned early in mid-July. By 1974 several were reported remaining for the entire summer. The species spread rapidly throughout the Phoenix area and assumed the status as a common resident. In 1994 a pair was observed in pine-oak habitat at the unusually high elevation of 7000 feet on Mt. Ord.

Costa's Hummingbird also nests during the winter months. Until the early seventies the species was not known to be present in the county during the summer. In 1972 a male remained for the entire summer at a feeder in Sun City. Since that time a few have remained each summer in a small number of yards in the greater Phoenix area.

Until the early seventies **Acorn Woodpecker** was considered only an irregular fall and winter wanderer in the county. Gradually, observations began to accumulate in spring and fall in the Superstition and Mazatzal Mountains, as well as on Four Peaks and Mt. Ord. Low elevation fall and winter records also increased. The first summer records were of several observed on Mt. Ord in 1992. The species has continued to nest there since that time, and may also be nesting on other mountains in the county.

Until recently, **Western Bluebird** was known only as a winter visitor in the county. The first nesting record was established in May 1991 when an adult was seen feeding young on Mt. Ord. There had been no previous spring or summer records in this well-birded area.

Rufous-backed Robin was not as rare in the county during the late sixties and seventies. The first county record was of one that was present in Carefree from November 1966 to February 1967. During the next seven years there were five more records. In 1975 there were four records in one year, and one more in 1977. Since that time there have been only three records, one each in 1982, 1990, and 1995. There have been a total of 14 county records.

It is difficult to believe there were no **European Starlings** in the state at one time – none until 1946. The first nest in the county and the state was found near Glendale in 1954. Three pairs were found nesting in woodpecker holes at the old River Ranch in 1955. By 1957 the species was widespread. In January 1958, 100,000 were estimated at Litchfield Park.

There was only one record of **Olive Warbler** in the county (on Four Peaks in 1969) before 1974 when the species began to be reported in the Mazatzal Mountains. None had been found during studies in this area in 1970 and 1971. At least 18 were counted in the Mazatzals above Slate Creek Divide in June 1975, and were presumed to be nesting. The species was not found on Mt. Ord until June 1990. In June 1992 nesting was confirmed there when immatures were observed with adults.

Although there were a few summer records of **Yellow-headed Blackbird** in the county, the species was not found nesting until 1982 along the Gila River west of Arlington. By 1991, additional nesting sites were found at Arlington, Citrus Valley, and Dendora Valley. In 1994, nesting was also observed at Powers Butte and the confluence of the Hassayampa and Gila Rivers. This is another species dependent upon cattail marshes.

Some of the earliest records of **Great-tailed Grackle** in the county were one plus two more near Peoria, May 15 and 29, 1953; one, then two more at the New River Ponds, June 4 and 27, 1954; and one at the Ramsey-Hazlett Pond, June 9, 1955. Twelve were reported at the Gainey Ranch in Scottsdale in April 1958, and three at the River Ranch in 1961. By 1970 the species was considered to be fairly common at Encanto Park, in farmyards in southwest Phoenix, and in most riparian areas. The species gradually became more common and began expanding into sub-urban neighborhoods in the eighties.

BIRDING AREAS
compiled by Pat Beall

PHOENIX AND SCOTTSDALE

1. Desert Botanical Garden, Phoenix Zoo, and Papago Park

These areas are located between McDowell Road and Van Buren Street on Galvin Parkway (a southern extension of 64th Street). The Desert Botanical Garden (north of the Zoo and Park) is one of the best places in Phoenix to see native desert birds, especially hummingbirds, and there is the added bonus in the many beautiful and unusual plants. For visitors with limited time, this is the most accessible birding area in Phoenix. Visitors are welcome to join the Monday morning bird walks led by knowledgeable Garden volunteers. They begin at 8 A.M. in winter and at 7 A.M. during June, July, and August. The Garden is open every day, except Christmas Day, from 8 A.M. to sunset, October through April, and from 7 A.M. to 10 P.M., May through September. Phone: (602) 941-1217. There is an admission fee.

Many wild ducks winter at the ponds in the Zoo and the Park just north of the Zoo, including an occasional Eurasian Wigeon and sometimes Black-bellied Whistling-Ducks. They are attracted by the generous food supply provided by the Zoo for its pinioned exotics. Bronzed Cowbirds can be found on the Zoo grounds year-round. A pair of Pied-billed Grebes, a pair of Harris' Hawks, Black-crowned Night-Herons, Green Herons, and Common Moorhens nest at the Zoo. The bird feeders on the Arizona Trail are good locations for observing hummingbirds. The Zoo is open every day, except Christmas Day, from 9 A.M. to 5 P.M., September through April, and from 7 A.M. to 4 P.M., May through Labor Day. Phone: (602) 273-1341. There is an admission fee.

Bendire's Thrashers have been found in Papago Park in the open desert area near Hunt's Tomb, and around the pond near Hunt's Tomb.

2. Squaw Peak Park

This park is located in the Phoenix Mountain Preserve. Take Squaw

PHOENIX AND SCOTTSDALE

1. Desert Botanical Garden, Phoenix Zoo, Papago Park
2. Squaw Peak Park
3. Phoenix South Mountain Park
4. Scottsdale

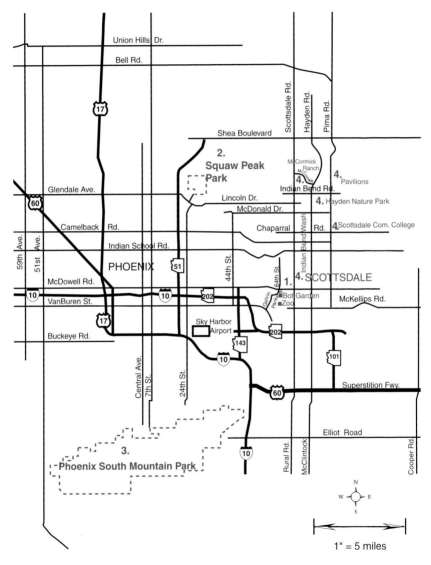

1" = 5 miles

Jak Keyser

Peak Drive north from Lincoln Drive, one mile west of 24th Street, and drive to the end of the paved road where there is a parking area. From here there is a trail that leads through the desert, giving birders the opportunity to see resident desert birds such as Canyon and Rock Wrens, Black-tailed Gnatcatchers, Black-throated Sparrows, and Canyon Towhees. It is possible to hear and see Elf Owls and Western Screech-Owls in early spring and summer, and to find Costa's Hummingbirds in winter and early spring.

3. Phoenix South Mountain Park

This is the largest city park in the United States. It is located south of the freeway at the south central edge of the city. From I-10, take the 7th Street Exit (Exit 195B) south for about 3 miles to Baseline Road, turn right for 0.5 mile to Central Avenue. Turn left and go south on Central Avenue for about 2 miles to the Park entrance. Most of the common desert birds can be seen here around the many picnic ramadas and along the hiking trails at the Summit Lookout.

4. Scottsdale

Frequently, visitors attending meetings at one of the Scottsdale resorts have only a limited amount of time for birding. Fortunately there is a surprising variety of birdlife within the Scottsdale city limits.

McCormick Ranch: With its ponds, golf course, and trees, this area attracts resident birds as well as wintering geese and ducks, and migrating water birds. Following is a clockwise loop route with five stops around the perimeter of the Ranch: From the intersection of Scottsdale and Camelback Roads, go north on Scottsdale Road for 2.5 miles past Indian Bend Road to the Radisson Resort on the right, at 7171 N. Scottsdale Road. Turn in and drive to the far northeast corner of the parking lot behind the Resort and park. Walk northeast out onto the grassy area and up onto a rise from which there is a view of the small cattail pond below. Among the interesting birds that have been found here are Common Snipe, Marsh Wrens, and sometimes a Vermilion Flycatcher. On the way to this area from the parking lot, look to the left along the row of oleander bushes where a resident Greater Roadrunner can usually be seen. Return to the car and drive north on Scottsdale

Road a short distance past the commercial buildings to the Regal McCormick Ranch Resort at 7401 N. Scottsdale Road. Turn right and drive to the northeast corner of the parking lot. From here there is a good view of the lake. A Ross' Goose has occasionally been found wintering here. Return to Scottsdale Road and drive the short distance to McCormick Parkway. Turn right and park in the restaurant parking lot on the right. From here there is another view of the lake as well as of the small entrance pond on the north side of McCormick Parkway. Walk across the Parkway for a closer view. A Eurasian Wigeon has been present off and on in this small pond during recent winters. Continue driving east on McCormick Parkway for about 0.5 mile to McCormick Ranch Golf Club at 7505 McCormick Parkway. Turn right into the parking lot and park. Walk south from the lot to the lake for another view of the lake as well as of the birds in the trees along the way. Next drive east on McCormick Parkway about 0.5 mile to Hayden Road. Turn right and go almost 1 mile south back to Indian Bend Road. Turn right, go about 0.5 mile until the lake is in view on the right. Pull well off the road. There are "No Parking" signs on either side of the road at this point, so in order to spend more than a few minutes here it will be necessary to drive forward a short distance to the hotel on the left, park in that parking lot, and walk back to the lake. This ends the loop of the Ranch.

Hayden Nature Park: From the lake at McCormick Ranch on Indian Bend Road, turn around and head east on Indian Bend Road back to Hayden Road. Turn right on Hayden. The small Nature Park is just north of the canal on the east side of the road. However, because the traffic is so heavy here, drive south to the next intersection, Lincoln Drive, turn right and around back to Hayden, turn left onto Hayden and drive 0.3 mile to the entrance to the Park on the right, immediately after crossing the canal. There is a trail through desert vegetation where most of the desert birds can be found. From the trail it is possible to look down into the flood-control greenbelt area on the north side of the trail where hawks and falcons are sometimes seen as well as the closest in-town views of wintering Horned Larks and American Pipits. There are rest rooms and benches in the Park.

Pavilions Shopping Center: Drive north on Hayden Road back to Indian Bend Road. Turn right and go east for 1 mile to Pima Road and drive into the shopping center. The ponds on either side of the entrance are worth checking. Drive to the far northeast corner of the shopping center and park. From here is a view of the golf course pond to the east of the shopping center. This pond attracts an interesting assortment of wintering geese, ducks, and other water birds. Behind the shopping center there is an open natural desert area (not yet developed as of this writing) where wintering sparrows and resident desert species can be found, including a Bendire's Thrasher occasionally.

Indian Bend Wash: There are two ponds along Hayden Road that are worth checking in winter for unusual water birds. One is on the east side of Hayden Road at Indian School Road (on both north and south sides). Indian School Road is 0.5 mile south of Camelback Road. A Greater Scaup has been recorded here more than once. The second pond is on the north side of McKellips Road, a short distance east of Hayden Road, in McKellips Lake Park. McKellips Road is 3 miles south of Indian School Road. The first Glaucous Gull record for the state was found on this pond.

Burrowing Owl: One of the most reliable places to find this species in the county is at Scottsdale Community College, located on Chaparral Road about 0.25 mile east of Pima Road. Chaparral Road is 0.5 mile north of Camelback Road. After turning left onto the entrance road into the College, begin looking immediately at the large grassy area on the right, where there are Burrowing Owl burrows among the Round-tailed Ground Squirrel burrows. The owls can also be found along the south end of the large parking lot on the left, around the edge of the small parking lot north of the college buildings, and in the athletic fields west of the main parking lot. They have even been seen perched on the newspaper stands on campus at dusk.

NORTHEAST OF PHOENIX

5. Fountain Hills and McDowell Mountain Park
6. Verde River north of Rio Verde
7. Verde River at Fort McDowell
8. Salt River between Granite Reef
   Dam and Saguaro Lake
9. Mesquite Wash, Sycamore Creek at
   Sunflower, Mt. Ord, Slate Creek Divide
10. Rackensack Gulch, Lower Camp Creek
    Humboldt Mt. Rd., Seven Springs

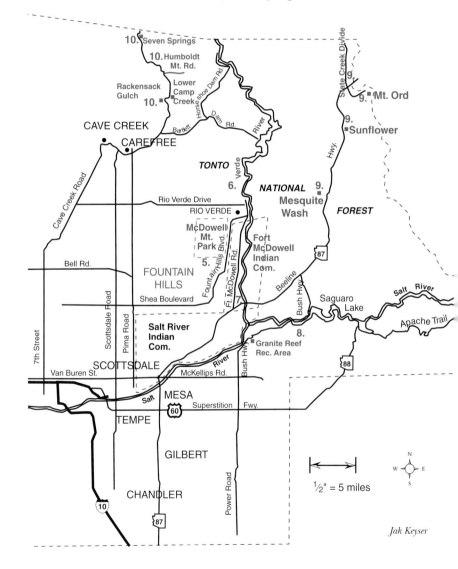

½" = 5 miles

Jak Keyser

NORTHEAST OF PHOENIX

5. Fountain Hills and Mcdowell Mountain Regional Park

Fountain Hills is located north of Shea Boulevard just west of the Beeline Highway (Route 87). From the intersection of either Scottsdale Road or Pima Road and Shea Boulevard, go east on Shea past Fountain Hills Boulevard to Saguaro Boulevard. Turn left (north) and drive 2.5 miles to the large lake with "The Fountain" at Saguaro and El Lago Boulevards. Check this lake in winter for ducks and grebes, including an occasional Horned Grebe. Harris' Hawks can often be seen while driving through the town. To reach McDowell Mountain Park from this point, turn left just north of the lake onto Palisades Boulevard for about 1.25 miles to Fountain Hills Boulevard, then right for about 2.5 miles to the Park entrance.

McDowell Mountain Park can also be reached by driving north from Shea Boulevard on Fountain Hills Boulevard (west of Saguaro Boulevard) approximately 7 miles to the Park entrance. There is a $2/car entrance fee, a fee campground, and many picnic areas. The camp hosts can provide a park map which shows all of the trails. This is a good place to see Harris' Hawks and Black-throated Sparrows, as well as other desert species. Western Screech-Owls and Great Horned Owls can be found here year-round. From late March through the summer, Elf Owls, Common Poorwills, and Lesser Nighthawks can be found. A Greater Roadrunner has been seen several times at dawn within the first 0.5 mile of the park entrance.

(Note: In July 1995, a lightning-caused fire burned 70% of the plants in the park, including many of the old saguaros. With the help of volunteers, re-vegetation is taking place, but it will be many years before the park will be restored to its former status.)

6. Verde River north of Rio Verde

After birding McDowell Mountain Park, continue north on Fountain Hills Boulevard, going through the town of Rio Verde where the road name changes to Forest Road. At the corner of Forest Road and Rio Verde Drive, turn right onto FR #160 and drive 0.5 mile. Park and walk down the hill to a mesquite bosque and riparian area. Bird both ways along the river. Crissal Thrashers have been found here. It is a good place to see hawks, owls, gnatcatchers, and Phainopeplas, as well as migrating and wintering flycatchers, vireos, and warblers.

Return to Forest Road and Rio Verde Drive, and drive north for 3 miles on FR #20 to Needle Rock, stopping at a large mesquite bosque on the way. Herons, egrets, Ospreys, hawks, shorebirds, and sometimes a Greater Roadrunner can be seen along the river.

7. Verde River at Fort McDowell Indian Community

Approximately 27 miles northeast of Phoenix, State Route 87 (Beeline Highway) crosses the Verde River. It is possible to bird several places along the river. From the intersection of Shea Boulevard and Route 87, drive northeast for 2 miles and turn left (north) at the light onto Fort McDowell Road. Go 1.2 miles to Mohave Road and turn right. At this point Mohave Road becomes Sandtrap Road. Drive 0.4 miles (keep left at the Y) to City of Phoenix Well No. 7. Park here and bird up and down the river. A scope would be helpful. Next, drive downstream (keep right at the Y) for about 1 mile and turn left (east) at City of Phoenix Well No. 9 onto a dirt road. Follow this road down to the river, past Well No. 8, and bird the area. Return on this road, An-Sha Lane, past Well No. 9 to the T intersection, turn right and drive the short distance to Fort McDowell Road. Turn left to return to Route 87.

This area is on the Fort McDowell Indian Community land, but birders are welcome. Along the river it is possible to find one or more pairs of resident Vermilion Flycatchers and is one of the best places to see Phainopeplas and Abert's Towhees. Harris' Hawks can often be seen in this area. In winter, look for Ospreys, Bald Eagles, and Common Mergansers. Bald Eagles and Bullock's Orioles nest here in spring, along with regular desert and riparian species. There is also a Great Blue Heron rookery in the area.

The agricultural fields are good places to observe raptors and sparrows in winter, and to look for Ruddy Ground-Dove which was recorded here once in winter. Drive north on Fort McDowell Road for 2.9

miles north of Mohave/Sandtrap Road (4.1 miles north of Route 87) to Ba Hon Na Road. Turn right and drive about 0.5 mile to the river. There are fields on both sides of this road. From the river either turn around and return to Fort McDowell Road, or turn right (south) onto Harquahala Road, a dirt road that runs between the river on the left and the fields on the right, and goes through a mesquite bosque. In about 2 miles Harquahala Road becomes an east-west road at City of Phoenix Well No. 3. Turn left for a short distance to reach the river, or turn right for a short distance to return to Fort McDowell Road.

8. Salt River between Granite Reef Dam and Saguaro Lake

From the Superstition Freeway (U.S. Route 60) take the Power Road exit and drive about 8 miles north to the Granite Reef Recreation Area. (Power Road becomes the Bush Highway farther north). There is a sign on the right and an almost hidden entrance on the left. This is a good birding area at any time of year, but especially in spring and fall migration. Bird the picnic grounds and down-river toward the dam.

Good birding is found all along the river as the road continues another 8 miles to Saguaro Lake. Choice spots are the recreation areas of Coon Bluff (there is usually a pair of Canyon Wrens nesting in the cliffs, and a Gray Flycatcher can sometimes be found in the mesquites in winter); Phon D. Sutton (a 2.5 mile nature trail circles through riparian and desert areas); and Blue Point Cottonwoods (very crowded in summer). About a mile beyond the turn-off to Saguaro Lake, turn right onto the road to Butcher Jones Recreation Site. It is located 2 miles down the road on an arm of Saguaro Lake. A 2.5 mile trail follows the shoreline. The first 0.25 mile to Peregrine Point is paved for wheelchair access. Picnic tables are situated adjacent to a mesquite bosque. Check these trees in winter for Gray Flycatchers and Brown Creepers, and in summer for Bell's Vireos and Lucy's Warblers.

All along the Salt River, look for Harris' Hawks and Bald Eagles.

Lesser Nighthawks can be seen at dawn in summer. In winter, check for loons, grebes, mergansers, and Ospreys.

This route can be run in reverse by driving northeast on Route 87, from the intersection with Shea Boulevard, for about 10 miles to the Bush Highway. Turn right and drive 2.8 miles to the road into Butcher Jones Recreation Site on the left.

9. Mesquite Wash, Sycamore Creek at Sunflower, Mt. Ord, and Slate Creek Divide

Travel northeast toward Payson on State Route 87 (Beeline Highway). Start with mile 0 at the intersection of Route 87 and Shea Boulevard. At 19.1 miles (about 0.7 mile beyond milepost 207) on the left is Mesquite Wash. This is a good spot to look for Zone-tailed Hawks, Ladder-backed Woodpeckers, Ash-throated and Brown-crested Flycatchers, Bell's Vireos, Lucy's Warblers, Yellow-breasted Chats, and migrating flycatchers, vireos, and warblers.

Continuing north on Route 87, at 29.5 miles on the right is the nonexistent town of Sunflower. At 30.1 miles turn right onto the dirt and gravel road signed "Bushnell Tank." Follow this road at least to the second stream crossing of Sycamore Creek, where birding is pleasant year-round among some fine old sycamores and other riparian vegetation, at an elevation of about 3200 feet. Weekends can be crowded. Cattle were removed from this area in 1993 (except during winter months), and already a dramatic recovery has taken place with new growth of riparian vegetation. In spring and summer, this is a good place to see Summer Tanagers, as well as flycatchers, vireos, warblers, and orioles that nest here. Cooper's and Zone-tailed Hawks and Common Black-Hawks have nested in this area.

Continue north on Route 87. At 35.4 miles (between mileposts 223 and 224) on the right is the hidden dirt road to the top of Mt. Ord, with its stop sign showing before the turn-off is visible. It is about 7 miles to the top of Mt. Ord at an elevation of 7100 feet. On the way up, 1.5 miles up the dirt road, pull off into the wide open area on the left and listen and look for Scott's Orioles (in summer), and Black-chinned, Rufous-crowned, and Black-throated Sparrows year-round. In spring and summer, walk back down the road to where the junipers and other vegetation are more dense, to listen and look for Gray Vireos.

Next, drive another 2.5 miles. On the right is a primitive road and a cattle-loading chute. Park here. On the left, seen while you walk down the road, is a hillside with several small springs and an open concrete water tank. Nesting Broad-tailed Hummingbirds, Hutton's Vireos, Virginia's Warblers, Black-throated Gray Warblers, Grace's Warblers, Painted Redstarts, and sometimes Olive Warblers can be found here. Continue driving for another 3 miles to the gate and park off the road. Do not drive through the gate even if it is open. Walk up the road beyond the gate toward the summit of Mt. Ord. In the higher-elevation pines and oaks near the top, look for Band-tailed Pigeons, Acorn and Hairy Woodpeckers, Western Bluebirds, Grace's Warblers, Olive Warblers, and Hepatic Tanagers. Just below the summit where the road traverses a more open and brushy hillside, look for nesting Blue-gray Gnatcatchers and Virginia's Warblers.

Back on Route 87, 1.3 miles beyond the turn-off to Mt. Ord, there is a large pull-off on the left for trucks. Toward the far end of the pull-off is a dirt road over a cattle guard. This area is known as Slate Creek Divide. Take the road uphill to an old corral. Gray Vireos, Rufous-crowned, Black-chinned, and Black-throated Sparrows, and Scott's Orioles nest in this area, especially in the drainage immediately below the corral. With luck a Crissal Thrasher may be found. Most of the birds can also be found in the first mile down the dirt road to the left after crossing the cattle guard. This road is signed "Mormon Grove Trailhead." The road beyond the corral requires a high clearance vehicle and leads to more higher-elevation pine forests with species similar to those found on Mt. Ord.

10. Rackensack Gulch, Lower Camp Creek, Humboldt Mt. Road, and Seven Springs

Seven Springs is 16.2 miles from the intersection of Pima Road and Cave Creek Road in Carefree. Starting with the intersection as 0, go northeast on Cave Creek Road. At 6.7 miles the pavement ends after a sharp left downhill curve. This dirt road is well maintained. At 9.3 miles on the left is a dirt road known as Rackensack Gulch. Park along the side of the main road so as not to block the Rackensack road. Birding along the first half-mile of Rackensack, it is possible to find Rufous-crowned and Black-chinned Sparrows as well as the more common chaparral species. Birding is also good along the wash across the road from Rackensack Gulch. Crissal Thrashers have been found in this area.

Continuing on the main road, drive to the 9.7-mile mark where there is an orange road sign on the right saying "Dips, Winding Rd." Turn right onto a small dirt road and park well off the road. Climb over or under the usually locked gate and bird down the road past the main stream crossing of sycamore-lined Camp Creek to the next stream crossing. This area is known as Lower Camp Creek. The property on each side of the road is private, so please stay on the road. Do not drive through the gate even if it is open as the gate is not left open or unlocked for long.

Back on the main road, continue to the road to Humboldt Mt. on the right at 13.9 miles. Western and Mountain Bluebirds, Townsend's Solitaires, and Sage Thrashers can often be found along this narrow paved road in winter and early spring. Gray Vireos and Scott's Orioles are found here in spring and summer. For a spectacular view, continue up the narrow, steep, single lane paved road to the microwave towers at the top.

Continuing on the main road, at 16.2 miles turn left at the second water crossing into the Seven Springs Picnic Area. There is a primitive restroom here. Bird the picnic area and the hillside. The area beyond the fence is private property. Weekends are usually crowded and noisy here, but there is a group "CCC" forest campground about 0.5 mile farther along the main road on the left that is more quiet if it is not being used. From this campground, walk across the main road onto a dirt road that parallels and overlooks another riparian area; this road ends, after a steep descent, at the stream. Do not attempt to go farther along the main road without a four-wheel-drive vehicle, a map, and normal desert survival supplies.

Both Lower Camp Creek and Seven Springs contain mature riparian vegetation and adjacent rocky, brushy hillsides. In the riparian areas, one may find Cooper's and Zone-tailed Hawks, Common Black-Hawks, Golden Eagles, Brown-crested Flycatchers, Bridled Titmice, Hooded Orioles, and Summer Tanagers in spring and summer; and migrating flycatchers, warblers, tanagers, and orioles in spring and fall. In spring, Rufous-crowned and Black-chinned Sparrows sing from the hillsides adjacent to the riparian areas and along the main road. Watch for Western Scrub-Jays along the main road, and look for Plain Titmice in juniper habitat around and beyond Seven Springs. Red-naped Sapsuckers and Townsend's Solitaires can be found in the area during some winters.

Burrowing Owls
Marilyn Hoff Stewart

SOUTHEAST OF PHOENIX

11. Tempe
12. Chandler Sewage Ponds
13. Sun Lakes Sewage Ponds and Gilbert/Riggs Ponds
14. Chandler
15. Gilbert Wildlife Area Ponds

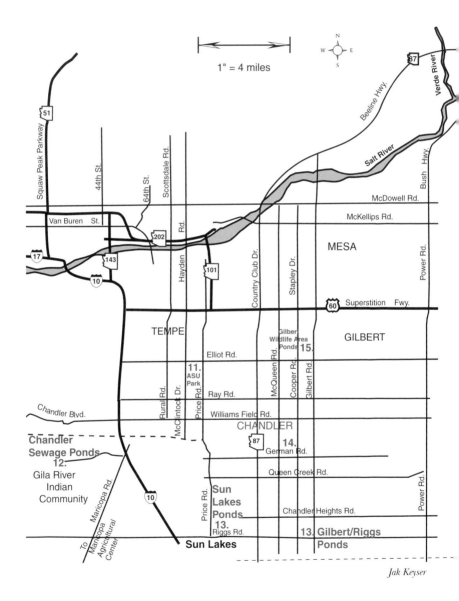

Jak Keyser

SOUTHEAST OF PHOENIX

11. Tempe

Arizona State University Research Park: This garden industrial park is located in Tempe south of Elliot Road between McClintock Drive and Price Road on River Parkway. The non-business areas of this attractive park are open to the public. There are several lakes along River Parkway that attract a variety of wintering ducks and a few shorebirds. Drive south on River Parkway to Research Drive. Turn left and park along the road and walk to the lakes on the east and west side of River Parkway. Do not park along River Parkway itself or in the parking areas of the private businesses. To check other lakes, continue south on River Parkway to a parking pull-off on the right across from Science Drive. You may also park along Science Drive. The park is bound on the south by Warner Road.

12. Chandler Sewage Ponds

Drive south on I-10, past Chandler Boulevard and exit at Maricopa Road South (Exit 162A). At the bottom of the exit ramp there is a cattle guard and a large dirt pull-off to the right. Turn right through the parking pull-off and follow the wide dirt road that bends first right and then left. At 2.8 miles is the chain link fence enclosing the sewage ponds on the left. The gate to these ponds is open on weekdays from 7 A.M. to 2 P.M. It is closed on Saturday and Sunday. Be sure to stop at the office to ask permission to bird the ponds. Also stop on the way out to let them know you are leaving.

There are two ponds, a lower and an upper. Drive to the far end of the ponds and check the southwest corner of the lower pond for shorebirds. Drive on the road up the slope to view the upper pond which is preferred by the ducks. A scope would be helpful. From November through March this pond attracts many wintering species of ducks. In the past an occasional pelican has dropped by and there is often an Osprey on top of one of the utility poles. Peregrine and Prairie Falcons are occasionally seen here.

The road to the sewage ponds passes through private land belonging to the Gila River Indian Community. You may view various desert birds from the car, but you are asked not to trespass.

13. Sun Lakes Sewage Ponds and Gilbert-Riggs Ponds

Go south of Phoenix on I-10 and exit east on Riggs Road (Exit 167) toward Sun Lakes for 1.5 miles. Turn left (north) on Price Road for about 0.5 mile and park on the right by the gate of the chain-link fenced sewage pond. The small ponds can be viewed through the fence (afternoon light is best), and are known mostly for the Black-bellied Whistling-Ducks that come and go all year. A few ducks, especially Cinnamon Teal, frequent the ponds in winter along with Black-necked Stilts. In summer American Avocets and Black-necked Stilts nest here.

Continue east on Riggs Road for 6 miles beyond Price Road to Gilbert Road. Turn left (north) on Gilbert Road for 0.2 miles. Two ponds on the left side of the road attract herons, ducks, and shorebirds.

14. Chandler

There is roughly a 6-square-mile area in this town that can produce some good birding in the fall, winter, and spring months. The area is bordered on the north by Ray Road, on the east by Gilbert Road, on the south by Chandler Heights Road, and on the west by Price Road. The habitat is predominantly agricultural fields, dairy farms, and a few small residential developments containing a number of small lakes. Swainson's Hawk migration in the fall can be noteworthy in some years. White-tailed Kites seem to prefer the northwest section of the area as does an occasional Ruddy Ground-Dove. Red-tailed, Ferruginous and, rarely, a Rough-legged Hawk dot the tops of the power poles. At the residential lakes, especially in the Ocotillo development (between Price and Alma School Roads, south of Queen Creek Road), there are usually Canada and Snow Geese and the usual wintering ducks, sometimes including Black-bellied Whistling-Ducks, Cinnamon Teal, perhaps Blue-winged Teal, and at times even a Eurasian Wigeon. Usually a Prairie Falcon can be found in this area. There is a Great Blue Heron colony in the Ocotillo development.

Yellow-headed Blackbirds can be found in winter at the dairy west of Price Road and Queen Creek Road, on Old Price Road. Ruddy Ground-Doves were found behind and along the edge of this dairy during one winter.

Burrowing Owls can be seen at the Chandler Municipal Airport. Drive east on Germann Road to Airport Boulevard, 0.5 mile beyond McQueen Road. Turn right and drive on Airport Boulevard past the executive terminal on the left to the open area on the left where there are many Round-tailed Ground Squirrel burrows. Look for the owls near the burrows and on the fence. There is a marshy area along the right side of Airport Boulevard where water birds can be seen. A second area at the airport can be reached by returning north on Airport Boulevard to Ryan Road. Turn right (east) on Ryan Road to Curtis Way, then right again. Look for the owls along the left side of Curtis Way where there are some ditches, pipes, and a fence.

15. Gilbert Wildlife Area Ponds

These ponds are located in the town of Gilbert near the intersection of Elliot and Cooper Roads. From this intersection go north on Cooper Road about 0.2 mile and turn right (east) into the parking lot of Gilbert Fire Station No. 215. Drive to the far end and park. A paved path ahead and to the left goes slightly uphill to a raised viewing area of several ponds. This path can accommodate wheel chairs. A scope would be helpful. The water level in the ponds fluctuates. However, during spring and fall migration, when pond conditions are right, mudflats attract a variety of shorebirds and White-faced Ibis. In winter, the fuller ponds will have several duck species, including Cinnamon Teal and sometimes Black-bellied Whistling-Ducks. Occasionally a wintering Peregrine Falcon is attracted to this area. Black-bellied Whistling-Ducks, Cinnamon Teal, Black-necked Stilts, and American Avocets nest here.

These ponds can be reached from I-10 by taking the Elliot Road exit, or from the Superstition Freeway, by taking the Stapley Road exit. Stapley Road becomes Cooper Road.

SOUTHWEST OF PHOENIX

16. 91st Avenue Wastewater Treatment Plant
17. El Mirage Pond
18. Farmfields and Feedpens
19. Estrella Mountain Regional Park
20. Le Conte's Thrasher Area
21. Robbins Butte, Powers Butte, Arlington Wildlife Areas
22. Painted Rock Dam
23. Gila Bend Sewage Ponds

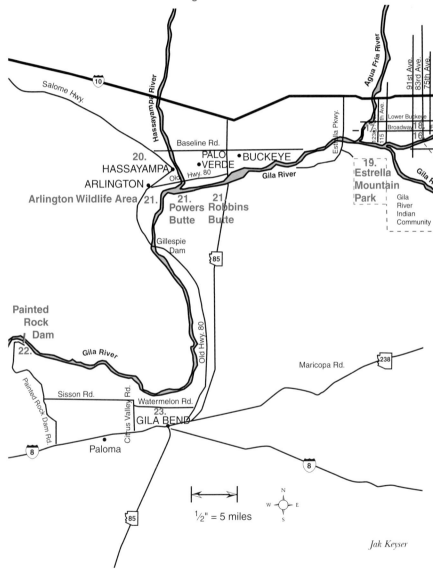

Jak Keyser

SOUTHWEST OF PHOENIX

16. 91st Avenue Wastewater Treatment Plant

This plant is the location of the new wetlands project ponds where marsh plants are used to help purify water and provide habitat for wildlife. The ponds parallel the riparian area of cottonwoods and willows that runs along the effluent channel from 91st Avenue to 83rd Avenue. From this area it is also possible to look down into the Salt River bed. A variety of birdlife can be expected from this combination of riparian, pond, marsh, and river habitat.

Drive west from Phoenix on I-10, exit at 91st Avenue (Exit 134), go 3.8 miles south to Broadway Road, then another 0.8 mile south to the entrance to the Plant on the left. From the entrance road into the plant, turn right immediately onto the first road to reach the office. It is necessary to go inside the office to obtain permission to visit the wetlands ponds, south and east of the main plant. The office opens at 7 A.M.

There are additional wetlands ponds on the west side of 91st Avenue. Drive 0.4 miles south of the plant entrance to a dirt parking area on the west side, where a sign says "City of Phoenix Property. No Trespassing." Birders have permission to park in this area. These ponds, north of the Salt River bed, also parallel the riparian area that borders the effluent channel running west of 91st Avenue.

To reach the El Mirage Pond from this point, drive north to Lower Buckeye Road (one mile north of Broadway), then west to 123rd Avenue.

17. El Mirage Pond

This is a holding pond for agricultural irrigation water. As such, the water level fluctuates often, from bone dry to very full. It is located in Avondale southwest of Phoenix on the west side of El Mirage Road (123rd Avenue), 0.5 mile south of Lower Buckeye Road. Drive west from Phoenix on I-10, exit at 115th Avenue (Exit 131), go about 2.5 miles south to Lower Buckeye Road, turn right (west) for 1 mile, then left onto El Mirage Road. After passing the buildings on the right, and immediately after Illini Street, drive up onto the embankment surrounding the pond and drive around the pond. Your vehicle makes a good blind.

This is another place where a Greater Roadrunner can be seen with some regularity, as well as shorebirds and a few ducks, including Black-bellied Whistling-Ducks. During the winter of 1990-91, this pond hosted four Ruddy Ground-Doves in with the Common Ground-Doves. Check the surrounding fields for a variety of sparrows and perhaps a Burrowing Owl. Check the power poles in the area for hawks in winter.

18. Farmfields and Feedpens

From the El Mirage Pond, return to Lower Buckeye Road, turn right and drive east on Lower Buckeye Road to 75th Avenue. Turn right, drive 1 mile south to Broadway Road, turn right (west) and return to 115th Avenue. Along this circle route are farm fields that are worth checking in winter for Ferruginous and Rough-legged Hawks, Prairie Falcons, and Short-eared Owls. Cattle Egrets, White-faced Ibis, and shorebirds can be found in flooded fields during irrigation. In winter Yellow-headed Blackbirds can be seen in the cattle feedpens in the area. Swainson's Hawks can be seen in these fields during spring and fall migration.

19. Estrella Mountain Regional Park

From I-10 west of Phoenix, take Exit 126 onto Estrella Parkway. Drive south for about 5 miles and cross the bridge over the Gila River. Although the riparian vegetation was washed out during the 1993 flood, it is recovering. Stop here and bird both sides of the bridge where it is possible to see Rock and Canyon Wrens, Abert's Towhees, wintering ducks, Common Moorhens, herons, egrets, Black-necked Stilts, and other riparian species. From the bridge, turn left and then right at the park entrance. Go east to the last parking area at the east end of the park. This is a very popular park and can be crowded on weekends. Here the Greater Roadrunner comes as close to being a sure thing as anywhere in the valley. Gilded Flickers can be found here, and in winter one can usually see one or two Gray Flycatchers, Red-naped Sapsuckers, Phainopeplas, and occasionally a Greater Pewee. The mesquites in the southeast corner of the park can be good for migrating warblers, vireos, and tanagers. Watch for a possible Prairie Falcon. At the west end of the park, a Crissal Thrasher can sometimes be found.

The park is open daily, except Christmas Day, from 6 A.M. to 7 P.M., Sunday through Thursday, and from 6 A.M. to 8 P.M., Friday and Saturday. There is a $2/car entrance fee.

20. Le Conte's Thrasher Area

Drive west on I-10 to Route 85 (Exit 112) and go south for about 3.8 miles to Baseline Road. Turn right (west) on Baseline Road for 8.5 miles to where it intersects with the Salome Highway (a T intersection). Turn left onto the Salome Highway and immediately pull off onto the right-hand shoulder of the road and park. Walk across the dilapidated barbed wire fence and walk straight ahead. The birds can be found within the next 100–200 yards as well as anywhere in the surrounding salt bush desert habitat, including the area on the opposite side of Salome Highway. LeConte's Thrashers are present in this habitat year-round, but are easiest to find January through March when they are nesting and males are singing. A tape recording of the song is helpful. This is also a good place to find Sage Sparrows in winter and migrating Sage Thrashers in March. Crissal and Bendire's Thrashers can be found in this area where the vegetation is more dense, especially in the washes.

21. Robbins Butte, Powers Butte, and Arlington Wildlife Areas

All three of these areas, managed by the Arizona Game and Fish Department, are located along the Gila River, southwest of Buckeye, about 30 miles west of Phoenix.

Robbins Butte: Drive west on I-10 to Route 85 (Exit 112). Go south for 8 miles on Route 85 to the entrance to Robbins Butte Wildlife Area on the right (1 mile south after crossing the Gila River). Turn right onto the dirt road. About 0.3 mile along this road there is a fork. The left fork leads to Powers Butte. The road straight ahead extends for about 2 miles into Robbins Butte Wildlife Area. This area has farm fields planted in grain crops and is a good place to visit during the winter to look for White-tailed Kites, Ferruginous Hawks, Prairie Falcons, and other raptors, as well as desert species, in the surrounding mesquite and creosote desert. Return toward Route 85 and take the dirt road on the right lead-ing to Powers Butte.

Powers Butte: The road to the Powers Butte Wildlife Area is a drive of approximately 6 miles, winding through private holdings and interesting desert areas. (This road becomes extremely muddy after rains). Most of the Wildlife Area is closed to vehicular traffic, but it is possible to travel on foot to the large cottonwood tree plantings at the north and south ends of the property and to the cattail pond just south of the south group of cottonwoods. The pond is approximately 1 mile south (to the left as you enter) from the Powers Butte entrance, and is a good place to look for rails and Yellow-headed Blackbirds. The grain fields in the area have been planted to attract geese, raptors, and Sandhill Cranes in winter.

Arlington: Return to Route 85 and go north for 1 mile across the bridge over the Gila River, then left (west) on Old U.S. 80 for 5 miles to the small town of Arlington. From the Arlington Post Office (on the left), go about a mile farther to Arlington School Road. Turn left and go about 2.5 miles to Desert Rose Road. Drive straight ahead on the dirt road that parallels a field for 0.5 mile to the Arlington Wildlife Area ponds and cattail marsh. This is a good place to find Cinnamon Teal, rails, and Yellow-headed Blackbirds.

A dirt road between the field and the wildlife area (turn left just before the wildlife area) leads to an overlook of the Gila River with its sand bars and small islands of cattails. Look for herons, ducks, and shorebirds in winter.

Gila Bend can be reached by driving south on Route 85 or Old Highway 80. About 7 miles south of Arlington on Old Highway 80 is the historic Gillespie Dam. Park on the far side of the bridge and walk down below the dam to bird the cattail marsh that has grown up there since the flood that broke through the dam in 1993.

22. Painted Rock Dam

The town of Gila Bend is about 70 miles southwest of Phoenix. The road to Painted Rock Dam is 15 miles west of Gila Bend on I-8 (Exit

102). It is about a 10-mile drive north from I-8 to the dam. Double-crested Cormorants, Black-crowned Night-Herons, and egrets nest here. The area attracts common as well as rare species of loons, grebes, pelicans, herons, raptors, shorebirds, gulls, and terns. Visitors must park near (but do not block) the locked gate and walk the short distance to the area below the dam. A scope would be helpful.

In years with heavy rains and subsequent flooding, a large amount of water collects above the dam and also provides mudflats that attract herons, shorebirds, gulls, and terns. Access to this area is from Citrus Valley Road, about 5 miles west of Gila Bend, on I-8 (Exit 111). Turn north and drive about 5 miles until the road makes a left turn and becomes Sisson Road. Sisson Road (some paved and some dirt sections) parallels the area above the dam from Citrus Valley Road to Painted Rock Dam Road. There are dirt roads running north from Sisson Road toward the area above the dam. The dirt roads in this area become *extremely* muddy after rains and should be attempted only with caution or not at all. Even four-wheel-drive vehicles have become mired down here.

In the desert and fields adjacent to the dam, it is possible to see White-tailed Kites, Burrowing Owls, and sometimes a LeConte's Thrasher year-round. It is a good place to see raptors and sparrows in winter.

23. Gila Bend Sewage Ponds

Three ponds, located west of Gila Bend on Watermelon Road, are worth checking in late summer, fall, winter, and spring for shorebirds. Take Logan Avenue north to Indian Road, turn right and go 0.1 mile to 307th Avenue, turn left and go 1 mile to Watermelon Road, turn left and go 1.8 miles to the ponds on the left (south) side of the road.

NORTHWEST OF PHOENIX

24. Thunderbird Park
25. Lake Pleasant Regional Park
26. Hassayampa River Preserve

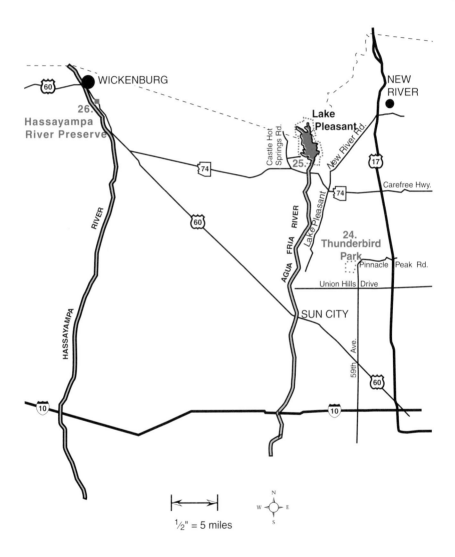

WICKENBURG

NEW RIVER

26.
Hassayampa
River Preserve

Lake
Pleasant

Castle Hot Springs Rd.

New River Rd.

25.

74

74

Carefree Hwy.

AGUA FRIA RIVER

Lake Pleasant

24.
Thunderbird
Park

Pinnacle Peak Rd.

Union Hills Drive

SUN CITY

RIVER

HASSAYAMPA

59th Ave.

½" = 5 miles

N W E S

Jak Keyser

NORTHWEST OF PHOENIX

24. Thunderbird Park

This smaller, fairly quiet park is located northwest of Phoenix on 59th Avenue, south of Pinnacle Peak Road. Take I-17 north to Union Hills Drive (Exit 213), go west to 59th Avenue, then north for 2 miles to the park. Among the usual desert birds, one can find Ladder-backed Woodpeckers, Curve-billed Thrashers, Black-throated Sparrows, often a Bendire's Thrasher, and possibly a Greater Roadrunner.

25. Lake Pleasant Regional Park

This new lake, formed by New Waddell Dam on the Agua Fria River, is about 35 miles northwest of Phoenix. Drive north on I-17 to the Carefree Highway, Route 74 (exit 223). Go west on Route 74 for about 7 miles, then northwest (right) on Route 74 for about 6 miles to Castle Hot Springs Road. Turn right and go about 2 miles to the entrance to Lake Pleasant Regional Park on the right. Another 4 miles beyond the entrance is a visitor center with an overlook that provides visitors with a view of the lake's main body near the dam. A scope would be helpful. There is a $1/person entrance fee.

Such a large body of water (almost 10,000 acres) should attract migrating pelicans, ducks, gulls, terns, and other water birds.

To reach the Hassayampa River Preserve south of Wickenburg, go west on Route 74 for another 23 miles to Highway 60/89, then northwest (right) for about 8 miles.

26. Hassayampa River south of Wickenburg

Wickenburg is about 51 miles northwest of Phoenix on U.S. Highway 60/89. The town is now home to The Nature Conservancy's "Hassayampa River Preserve." The entrance is 3 miles south of Wickenburg on the west side of the highway near milepost #114. In addition to the area around the Nature Shop, there are two trails for birding: the Lakeside Trail and the River Trail. Birding is pleasant and productive at all seasons, affording the opportunity to see the many species that inhabit a mature cottonwood/willow riparian forest. This is the best place in the county to see Yellow-billed Cuckoos. Harris' Hawks and Ruddy

Ground-Doves have nested here. A checklist is available at the Visitor Center. The Preserve is open from Wednesday through Sunday (closed Monday and Tuesday). Winter hours (September 16 to May 14) are from 8 A.M. to 5 P.M.; summer hours are from 6 A.M. to 12 noon. Closed Thanksgiving and Christmas. A $5 donation is suggested for nonmembers. Phone: (520) 684-2772.

A Roadside Rest stop is located about two miles southeast of the Preserve along the Hassayampa River on the west side of Highway 60/89. Although this is a busy place, it is usually a favorite nesting spot for a pair of Vermilion Flycatchers, as well as for other riparian species.

PINAL COUNTY

Not far from Phoenix are three popular birding areas outside of Maricopa County in Pinal County. (See County Map inside back cover).

27. Boyce Thompson Arboretum

Many rare and accidental species have been discovered here, including a Rufous-backed Robin. The Arboretum is located about 55 miles east of the center of Phoenix on U.S. Route 60, west of Superior. Go east on the Superstition Freeway through Mesa to Apache Junction. Continue east on U.S. 60 for about 28 miles to the sign for the Arboretum on the right. The Arboretum is now a State Park and is always worth a visit, especially during winter and spring. A checklist is available at the Visitor Center. The bird life among the many arid-land plants and along Queen Creek is varied, with species from both mountains and desert. Habitats include desert, riparian, rocky cliffs, and a small lake. Hours are from 8 A.M. to 5 P.M. daily except Christmas Day. There is an entrance fee. Phone: (520) 689-2811.

The birding is most productive by starting at 8 A.M. and birding the picnic area and the creek trail before others walk the trails. This is a good place to see Soras (on Ayer Lake) and Red-naped Sapsuckers in winter. Zone-tailed Hawks can be seen in spring and summer. Harris' Hawks, White-throated Swifts, Anna's Hummingbirds, Canyon and Rock Wrens, and Canyon Towhees are among the interesting species to be found year-round.

HASSAYAMPA RIVER PRESERVE

Phone (520) 684-2772

49614 Highway 60   Wickenburg, AZ 85390

Open Wednesday thru Sunday *

Winter Hours (September 16 thru May 14)

Visitor Center — 8:00 a.m. to 5:00 p.m.
Trails — 8:00 a.m. to 4:30 p.m.

Summer Hours (May 15 thru September 15)

Visitor Center — 8:00 a.m. to 12:00 noon
Trails — 6:00 a.m. to 11:30 a.m.

* Preserve closed on these holidays
Thanksgiving Day & day after Thanksgiving
Christmas Eve day & Christmas Day
New Years Eve day & New Years Day

Note: Trails may be closed for various reasons including flooding, bird nesting, and fire hazard.
Please contact the Preserve for current status of the trails.

28. Lost Dutchman State Park

This is a beautiful desert park at the base of the Superstition Mountains, east of Mesa and Apache Junction. From Apache Junction take State Route 88 (Apache Trail) northeast for 5 miles to the Park entrance on the right. There is an admission charge. The Park opens at 8 A.M. but the gate is never closed, so it is possible to go earlier. Here, there are restrooms, picnic areas, and a campground. Most of the common desert birds can be found in this park, including Costa's Hummingbirds in winter and early spring.

Before paying the entrance fee, park in the visitor parking lot and walk the interpretive trail. Along the way there is a bench for viewing a bird feeder and a small ground-level bird bath. One of the few reliable places to find Pyrrhuloxias in the Phoenix area is at this feeder. Be careful with the identification as Northern Cardinals are common here. Once inside the Park there is another viewing bench, bird feeder, and a much larger water hole on the Discovery Trail between the Day Use Area and the Campground. A pair of Gilded Flickers nests in this area, and many birds come to bathe and drink.

29. Maricopa Agricultural Center

This is a large area consisting of fields, tree groves, and fish ponds, located 6 miles south of the county line. Take I-10 south and exit at Maricopa Road South (Exit 162A). Drive south on Maricopa Road for 11 miles to Casa Blanca Road. A small green sign on the right points to the Maricopa Agricultural Center; a sign on the left points to the Stoneville Seed Plant. Turn left and drive 2 miles to Sacate Road. Turn right (south) and drive 1 mile to the next intersection. There is a long pond partially encircled with cattails on the southeast corner of this intersection. Turn left, then immediately right to drive along the back edge of this pond. This is a good place to look for Yellow-headed Blackbirds and Marsh Wrens during fall, winter, and spring. Return to Sacate Road and continue south for 2 miles to Smith Enke Road. South of this intersection on the east side are two fish ponds worth checking.

Return to Smith Enke Road and turn right (east) for 0.2 mile to the Agricultural Center Headquarters Building on the left, where an informational brochure can be obtained. There are restrooms here.

From the Headquarters, return west on Smith Enke Road past Sacate Road for 1 mile to White Parker Road. Between Sacate and White Parker Roads are three more fish ponds on the right. There is a large pistachio tree grove on the southwest corner of Smith Enke and White Parker Roads, worth checking anytime, but especially during migration, for flycatchers, vireos, and warblers.

Common Ground-Doves can be seen along the edges of the surrounding farm fields. Look for Ruddy Ground-Doves among them. This is a good place to see wintering raptors and sparrows, Swainson's Hawks and Long-billed Curlews during migration, and Greater Roadrunners year-round.

Continue west on Smith Enke Road to return to Maricopa Road.

The Agricultural Center can be reached from the Gilbert/Chandler/ Sun Lakes area by driving west on Riggs Road past I-10 to Maricopa Road and then south. The Center can be reached from the south by taking the Casa Blanca Road exit (Exit 175) from I-10 and driving west on Casa Blanca Road to Sacate Road.

> Wherever you bird, be sure to put valuables out of sight and lock the car. Take extra water in the car, especially in summer.

Costa's Hummingbird
Kenn Kaufman

A BIRDING CALENDAR FOR MARICOPA COUNTY

compiled by Tom Gatz

JANUARY

Scan the tops of tall downtown Phoenix office buildings for wintering Peregrine and/or Prairie Falcons, and the more common White-throated Swifts. Check the farm fields southeast and southwest of Phoenix for White-tailed Kites, Ferruginous and Rough-legged Hawks, and Short-eared Owls. Check ponds and lakes for unusual geese and ducks. Visit Painted Rock Dam to look for loons and gulls. This is a good time to listen to and observe our resident thrashers (especially Le Conte's) as they begin singing. Courtship flights of Costa's Hummingbirds are in full swing.

FEBRUARY

Cinnamon Teal begin migrating up from Mexico. Other wintering ducks on ponds in the area are coming into breeding plumage and offer good observation and photo opportunities. Try the ponds at Papago Park, Phoenix Zoo, McCormick Ranch, Fountain Hills, Dobson Ranch (in Mesa), and Sun Lakes where they have become accustomed to people. Great Horned Owls and Costa's Hummingbirds are nesting. Bald Eagles begin nesting along rivers and lakes. Enjoy them from a distance to avoid disturbance. Now through the summer, help with the Arizona Breeding Bird Atlas project (until 1999) coordinated by the Arizona Game and Fish Department.

MARCH

Northern Rough-winged and Cliff Swallows are nesting. Other swallow species are in migration. Loggerhead Shrikes and most of the resident thrashers are nesting. Black-chinned Hummingbirds and

Hooded Orioles return. Check farm fields and ponds in the southeast and southwest part of the county for migrating White-faced Ibis and Long-billed Curlews. Observe Turkey Vultures carefully to look for Zone-tailed Hawks. Both Zone-tailed Hawks and Common Black-Hawks can be seen in migration along the Verde River. Later in the month listen for singing territorial Bell's Vireos, and Lucy's and Yellow Warblers in riparian areas.

APRIL

Best month to observe landbird spring migration. White-winged Doves return. Visit McDowell Mountain Park or Rio Verde at dusk and/or after dark to hear and see Western Screech-Owls, Elf and Great Horned Owls, as well as Common Poorwills and Lesser Nighthawks. Check plowed fields for flocks of migrating Swainson's Hawks. Remember the Nongame Checkoff on your tax return. Support the local Birdathon.

MAY

Breeding is in full swing at lower elevations. Listen to the dawn chorus. Songbirds migrating to the north are still passing through. A good place to see and hear both migrant and resident birds is on the lower Salt and Verde Rivers, east of Phoenix, and at The Nature Consevancy's Hassayampa River Preserve south of Wickenburg. Consider joining The Conservancy to help fund important habitat protection projects.

JUNE

Bird activity drops off quickly after dawn in the desert. Good time to study immature plumages of recently fledged birds. Take a trip up to cooler Mt. Ord to see and hear the higher elevation nesting species. Check ponds and mudflats at the end of the month for early returning shorebirds.

JULY

Check ponds and mud flats for early shorebirds, and wooded areas for first "fall" warblers. Visit Painted Rock Dam to see nesting cormorants, herons, and egrets, as well as early shorebirds, gulls, terns, and post-breeding wandering pelicans. Listen and look for late-nesting Yellow-billed Cuckoos in desert riparian areas. Check hummingbird feeders for migrating Rufous Hummingbirds now through September.

AUGUST

Shorebird and warbler "fall" migration underway. Visits to ponds and wooded areas can be productive, especially immediately after storms. Visit Painted Rock Dam for post-breeding wandering pelicans, herons, gulls, and terns, as well as migrating shorebirds. Belted Kingfishers return for the winter at the end of the month, along streams and canals.

SEPTEMBER

Monthly Audubon Society meetings begin the first Tuesday, 7:30 P.M., Phoenix Zoo, through April. Shorebird migration continues. Best month to observe fall migration of many landbirds. Watch for uncommon Vaux's Swifts overhead. Hawk and Osprey migration begins and continues into the fall. Check from north-south ridge tops where soaring birds of prey and vultures follow thermals in the late morning and afternoon. Look for groups of migrating Swainson's Hawks in fields southeast and southwest of Phoenix.

OCTOBER

Wintering sparrows and blackbirds arrive. Check isolated patches of trees in desert or agricultural areas which can become "vagrant traps" where an unusual eastern warbler can sometimes be found. Continue checking ponds and mudflats for shorebirds. Some of the rarest shorebirds have been found this month.

NOVEMBER

Check lakes for loons, grebes, gulls, and diving ducks. Visit city ponds for wintering waterfowl. Check American Wigeon flocks for Eurasian Wigeon. Drive roads in agricultural areas southeast and southwest of Phoenix for wintering birds of prey and shrikes on power poles. Storms at the end of the month sometimes blow in unusual water birds such as scoters and Heermann's Gulls.

DECEMBER

Assist with the Salt/Verde River, Gila River, Hassayampa River, and Carefree Christmas Counts. Check flocks of White-crowned Sparrows for uncommon White-throated, Golden-crowned, and Harris' Sparrows. Double-check the common Yellow-rumped Warblers for other warbler species. Unusual loons, cormorants, and gulls may turn up at Painted Rock Dam. Some Anna's Hummingbirds begin to nest.

Phainopepla
Marilyn Hoff Stewart

Species Accounts
and
Bar Graphs

This annotated checklist includes abundance, distribution, and preferred habitat of the species recorded in the region. The taxonomy and nomenclature follow the Sixth Edition of the A.O.U. Checklist of North American Birds and subsequent supplements.

Records are current to January 1996.

EXPLANATION OF BAR CHARTS

▬▬▬   Abundant — present in large numbers.

■■■■■   Irregular Abundant — irregularly present, sometimes abundantly.

▬▬▬   Common — present in moderate numbers; always seen.

─────   Fairly Common — present in small numbers; not always seen.

- - - - - - Uncommon — present in low numbers; seldom seen.
             or
             Irregular — present some years, absent in others.

·········   Rare — always a surprise, but not out of normal range.
             or
             Casual — out of normal range; four records or more.

· · ·   Accidental — far from normal range; fewer than four records.

~~~~~~   Extended stay of one or more birds in one or more years.

N   Known to nest in Maricopa County.

NF   Known to have nested formerly in Maricopa County.

N-1, N-2, N-3   Has nested once (N-1), twice (N-2), or three times (N-3) in Maricopa County, but not expected to nest on a regular basis.

EXPLANATION OF TEXT CHARTS

Habitats:

When we speak of habitats or Life Zones, we are referring to areas characterized by certain plants. As elevation changes, there also occurs a change in the type of vegetation.

Starting with the lowest elevation, the **Lower Sonoran Zone**, from 1000 to 4000 feet, is characterized by such plants as saguaro cactus, creosote bush, and palo verde, ironwood, and mesquite trees. Indicators of the **Upper Sonoran Zone**, from 4000 to 6000 feet, are juniper and pinyon pine trees, scrub oak and manzanita bushes (chaparral), and grassland. Indicators of the **Transition Zone**, found above 6000 feet on Mt. Ord and the Mazatzal Mountains, are ponderosa pine and Gambel's oak trees, and a small amount of Douglas fir trees in the colder north-facing canyons.

When we speak of **Riparian** vegetation, habitats, or ecosystems, we are referring to areas that are associated with bodies of water (streams or lakes), or areas that are dependent on the existence of perennial, inter-mittent, or ephemeral surface or subsurface water drainage. This habitat, found at every elevation, contains a higher density of avian species be-cause of the water and more dense and varied vegetation (providing food, cover, and nesting sites) than in other habitats. Typical trees of this habitat are cottonwood, willow, sycamore, ash, walnut, and mesquite.

Canals mentioned in the text refer to the Salt River Project irrigation canals that run throughout the metropolitan areas. Aqueducts men-tioned in the text refer to the Central Arizona Project aqueducts which bring water from the Colorado River to central Arizona, then south to Tucson. Since the aqueduct from the Colorado River was completed to Phoenix in the fall of 1985, it has provided a corridor for water birds to travel from the Colorado River to Maricopa County.

SPECIES ACCOUNTS – ABBREVIATIONS

Collections:

AMNH – American Museum of Natural History, New York

ARP – Allan R. Phillips Collection, Mexico

ASU – Arizona State University, Tempe

JSW – Johnson-Simpson-Werner Collection, Prescott College, Prescott

REA – Amadeo M. Rea Collection, San Diego

UA – University of Arizona, Tucson

USNM – United States National Museum, Washington, D.C.

Observers:

LA	Louis Armstrong	RF	Richard Ferguson
CB	Charles Babbitt	SF	Steven Flowers
JB	Jack Bartley	DF	Dan Fritz
PB	Pat Beall	SG	Steve Ganley
WB	Wade Beall	AG	Alan Gast
GB	Greg Beatty	TG	Tom Gatz
HB	Harvey Beatty	RG	Richard Glinski
CBe	Chuck Berginc	DG	David Griffin
MB	Mary Bonnewell	KG	Kathy Groschupf
MBd	Marian Bound	PH	Paul Hardy
RB	Robert Bradley	LH	Liz Hatcher
DB	Dave Brown	JH	Jim Hentz
BB	Bonnie Burch	MH	Marita Hornbaker
SB	Scott Burge	SH	Sandy Hornbaker
JBu	Jim Burns	VH	Vic Householder
BC	Bruce Campbell	TH	Todd Hull
LC	Laurie Cleary	CH	Chuck Hunter
AC	Ardis Collister	KI	Kathy Ingram
TC	Troy Corman	MJ	Marty Jakle
H&RC	Harry & Ruth Crockett	RJ	Roy Johnson
DD	Doug Danforth	JJo	Jill Jones
SD	Salome Demaree	RJo	Roy Jones
LD	Liscum Diven	CK	Chuck Kangas
ME	Mike Edwards	DK	Dan Kaplan
DFe	David Feese	KK	Kenn Kaufman

Observers: (Cont.):

JK	Junea Kelly	KR	Ken Rosenberg
BK	Beth Kolson	CR	Cal Royall
ML	Mark Larson	MS	Myron Scott
AL	Andy Laurenzi	LS	Linwood Smith
HL	Helen Longstreth	DS	David Stejskal
KM	Kathy Majlinger	TS	Tom Stejskal
SM	Stan Majlinger	CS	Curt Stensrude
AM	Abe Margolin	DSz	Doug Stotz
HM	Henry Messing	PS	Paul Sunby
RM	Robert Mesta	ST	Scott Terrill
GMc	Guy McCaskie	CTh	Carole Thickstun
GMe	Graham Metson	DT	Dick Todd
GM	Gale Monson	CT	Carl Tomoff
MM	Michael Moore	DTu	Don Turner
RN	Robert Norton	BT	Bill Tweit
LO	Lawrence Ormsby	AV	Anita Van Auken
DP	Dave Pearson	HW	Hugh Willoughby
KRa	Kurt Radamaker	JW	Janet Witzeman
ER	Eleanor Radke	RW	Robert Witzeman
AR	Amadeo Rea	JY	Josephine Yoba
JR	Jerry Rodgers		
GR	Gary Rosenberg	m. ob.	many observers

General:

B. of A. — Record taken from *The Birds of Arizona* by Allan Phillips, Joe Marshall, and Gale Monson. 1964. The University of Arizona Press, Tucson.

imm.– immature

juv. — juvenile

Red-throated Loon – Brown Booby

Species	Nest	Jan.	Feb.	Mar.	Apr.	May	June	July	Aug.	Sept.	Oct.	Nov.	Dec.
Red-throated Loon													
Pacific Loon													
Common Loon													
Yellow-billed Loon													
Pied-billed Grebe	N												
Horned Grebe													
Eared Grebe	N-1												
Western Grebe	N												
Clark's Grebe													
White-tailed Tropicbird													
Red-billed Tropicbird													
Blue-footed Booby													
Brown Booby													

Legend:

Abundant	▬▬▬
Irreg. Abund.	▪▪▪▪
Common	———
Fairly Com.	———
Uncom. or Irreg.	- - -
Rare or Casual	·········
Accidental	•
Ind. Extended Stay	~~~

Red-throated Loon – Brown Booby

Red-throated Loon	Accidental. Nov. 26, 1978 {1}, Painted Rock Dam [ST, GR]. Jan. 13, 1993 {1}, Painted Rock Dam [TC].
Pacific Loon	Casual transient and winter visitor; Painted Rock Dam and CAP Aqueduct, plus one old specimen record n. of Phoenix, Oct. 20, 1951 [ASU].
Common Loon	Fairly common transient, uncommon winter visitor; lakes, ponds, and aqueducts.
Yellow-billed Loon	Accidental. Jan. 15 – Feb. 11, 1984 {1}, Painted Rock Dam [CB, DS, RF *et al.*, photo JW].
Pied-billed Grebe	Fairly common summer resident, common winter visitor; lakes, ponds, streams, and canals.
Horned Grebe	Rare transient and winter visitor; lakes and ponds.
Eared Grebe	Abundant transient and winter visitor on larger lakes. Common winter visitor, rare summer visitor on smaller lakes and ponds. One nesting record: May 31, 1992 {adult with 3 young}, Gila Farms Pond [PS].
Western Grebe	Fairly common transient and winter visitor on lakes. Uncommon transient and winter visitor on ponds and lagoons. Irregular breeding summer resident at Painted Rock Dam.
Clark's Grebe	Uncommon transient and winter visitor. Only recent records. Some older records of "Western" Grebe may pertain to this species.
White-tailed Tropicbird	Accidental. Aug. 22, 1980 {found exhausted and died}, Scottsdale [KI]; specimen [USNM].
Red-billed Tropicbird	Accidental. Apr. 10, 1905 {found exhausted and died}, near Phoenix [*fide* GM]; specimen [AMNH].
Blue-footed Booby	Accidental. July 29, 1953 {1}, Phoenix; specimen [ARP].
Brown Booby	Accidental. Sept. 14 – Oct. 11, 1990 {imm.}, Desert Harbor Lakes, n.w. Phoenix [DF *et al.*, photos TG, GR].

Braces, { }, denote number of individuals, etc.   Brackets, [ ], denote observers or institutions

American White Pelican – Reddish Egret

Species	Nest	Jan.	Feb.	Mar.	Apr.	May	June	July	Aug.	Sept.	Oct.	Nov.	Dec.
American White Pelican		····	····							····	····	····	····
Brown Pelican		····	····	····	····	····	····	····	····	····	····	····	····
Double-crested Cormorant	N						– – –						
Neotropic Cormorant		····	····	····	····	····	····	····	····	····	····	····	····
Magnificent Frigatebird								····	····				
American Bittern		····	····	····	····	····				·			····
Least Bittern	N	·		~~~	~~~	····	····			····		·	·
Great Blue Heron	N	▬▬▬	▬▬▬	▬▬▬	▬▬▬	▬▬▬	▬▬▬	▬▬▬	▬▬▬	▬▬▬	▬▬▬	▬▬▬	▬▬▬
Great Egret	N	– – –	– – –	───	───	– – –	───	───	───	───	───	– – –	– – –
Snowy Egret	N	– – –	– – –	───	───	───	───	───	───	───	───	– – –	– – –
Little Blue Heron		~			·	····	····	····	····				
Tricolored Heron						·	·	~	·	~	·	~	
Reddish Egret											·		

Legend:

▬▬▬ Abundant	Common	─ ─ ─ Uncom. or Irreg.	· · · Accidental
▬ ▬ ▬ Irreg. Abund.	Fairly Com.	········· Rare or Casual	~~~ Ind. Extended Stay

American White Pelican – Reddish Egret

Species	Description
American White Pelican	Uncommon transient (sometimes in large numbers), rare winter and summer visitor; lakes and ponds. Fairly common locally at Painted Rock Dam in late summer, fall, and winter.
Brown Pelican	Uncommon summer and fall visitor (most are immatures), with a few remaining through winter and rarely into spring; lakes and ponds.
Double-crested Cormorant	Fairly common transient and winter visitor; lakes, ponds, streams, and aqueducts. Has nested at Painted Rock Dam sporadically since 1979.
Neotropic Cormorant	Casual visitor. Records from Painted Rock Dam, Gillespie Dam, Granite Reef Dam, and 35th Ave. Phoenix ponds.
Magnificent Frigatebird	Casual late summer to early fall visitor. Majority of records from Painted Rock Dam.
American Bittern	Rare transient and winter visitor; marshy areas.
Least Bittern	Rare transient and local summer resident, a few winter records; cattail marshes.
Great Blue Heron	Common resident; lakes, ponds, streams, canals, and marshes. Nest rookeries on Verde and lower Salt Rivers, on the Agua Fria River above Lake Pleasant, and at Painted Rock Dam.
Great Egret	Fairly common transient, uncommon winter visitor, and irregular summer resident; ponds, streams, and marshes. Has nested at Painted Rock Dam in recent years.
Snowy Egret	Fairly common transient, uncommon winter visitor, and irregular summer resident; ponds, streams, and marshes. Has nested at Painted Rock Dam in recent years.
Little Blue Heron	Casual spring and summer visitor; streams and marshes.
Tricolored Heron	Casual spring and fall visitor; lakes, ponds, and streams.
Reddish Egret	Accidental. July 14–18, 1980 [imm.], Ahwatukee, Phoenix [?B *et al.*, photos CH, ST, RW]. Oct. 10, 1988 [imm.], Painted Rock Dam [SG *et al.*].

Braces, { }, denote number of individuals, etc.   Brackets, [ ], denote observers or institutions

Cattle Egret – Brant

Species	Nest	Jan.	Feb.	Mar.	Apr.	May	June	July	Aug.	Sept.	Oct.	Nov.	Dec.
Cattle Egret	N		-	-	-	-	-	-	-	-	-	-	-
Green Heron	N												
Black-crowned Night-Heron	N												
White Ibis						~~	•						
White-faced Ibis		-	-	-	-	▬	▬	▬	▬	▬	-	-	-
Roseate Spoonbill							••••	••••	••••	••••	•		
Wood Stork						••••	••••	••••	••••	••••			
Fulvous Whistling-Duck					•			~~~	~~~	~~~	~~~		
Black-bellied Whistling-Duck	N	▮	▮	▮	▮	▮	▮	▮	▮	▮	▮	▮	▮
Tundra Swan		••••	••••	••••	•							••	•••
Greater White-fronted Goose		••••	••••	••••	•	•						••	
Snow Goose		-	-	-		•	•		•	•			
Ross' Goose		••••	••••	••••	••••						-	••••	
Brant		••											~

Legend:

▬▬▬ Abundant	Common	- - - - - Uncom. or Irreg.
▮▮▮ Irreg. Abund.	——— Fairly Com.	••••••••• Rare or Casual

• • Accidental	
~~ Ind. Extended Stay	

Cattle Egret – Brant

Cattle Egret	Uncommon fall, winter, and spring visitor; rare summer visitor; fields, pastures, and ponds. Nested at Painted Rock Dam, summer 1993.
Green Heron	Fairly common resident; lakes, ponds, streams, marshes, and canals.
Black-crowned Night-Heron	Fairly common resident; lakes, ponds, marshes, and streams. Locally abundant in winter roosting areas.
White Ibis	Accidental. May 3–14, 1977 {10}, Verde River below Horseshoe Dam [BC *et al.*, photos DT, JW]. June 4, 1977 {1}, Hassayampa River, s. of Wickenburg [ST, AG].
White-faced Ibis	Common transient, uncommon summer visitor, and irregularly uncommon winter visitor; lakes, ponds, streams, marshes, and fields.
Roseate Spoonbill	Casual visitor, late summer to early fall; ponds, streams, and reservoirs.
Wood Stork	Rare, irregular visitor, late summer to early fall; ponds, marshes, and reservoirs. Majority of records from Painted Rock Dam.
Fulvous Whistling-Duck	Casual visitor from spring to early winter; ponds. Some records may pertain to escapees.
Black-bellied Whistling-Duck	Common local resident; ponds.
Tundra Swan	Casual winter visitor; lakes, ponds, and streams.
Greater White-fronted Goose	Uncommon fall transient and irregular rare winter visitor; lakes, ponds, and fields.
Snow Goose	Uncommon winter visitor; lakes and ponds.
Ross' Goose	Rare but regular winter visitor in small numbers; lakes and ponds.
Brant	Accidental. Jan. 6, 1975 {adult shot by hunter}, near Arlington [*fide* TS]. Dec. 11–14, 1991 {1}, Verde River, Ft. McDowell Indian Community [WB, PB *et al.*]. Jan. 7, 1992 {1}, Sun Lakes, s. of Phoenix [photos, MS].

Braces, { }, denote number of individuals, etc.	Brackets, [ ], denote observers or institutions

Canada Goose – Ring-necked Duck

Species	Nest	Jan.	Feb.	Mar.	Apr.	May	June	July	Aug.	Sept.	Oct.	Nov.	Dec.
Canada Goose	N												
Wood Duck													
Green-winged Teal													
Mallard	N												
Northern Pintail													
Blue-winged Teal	N-1												
Cinnamon Teal	N												
Northern Shoveler													
Gadwall													
Eurasian Wigeon													
American Wigeon													
Canvasback													
Redhead													
Ring-necked Duck	N-1												

Legend:
- ▬ Abundant
- ▰▰▰ Irreg. Abund.
- ▬ Common
- — Fairly Com.
- ----- Uncom. or Irreg.
- ·········· Rare or Casual
- · Accidental
- ~~~ Ind. Extended Stay

Canada Goose – Ring-necked Duck

Canada Goose	Common local winter visitor, rare summer visitor; lakes, ponds, and fields. Nesting records since 1992.
Wood Duck	Uncommon transient and winter visitor, with numbers increasing in winter; ponds, streams, and canals. Summer records may pertain to birds released by Phoenix Zoo.
Green-winged Teal	Common (locally abundant) transient and winter visitor, rare summer visitor; lakes, ponds, and streams.
Mallard	Common transient and winter visitor, rare summer resident (some nesting records pertain to feral birds); lakes, ponds, streams, and canals.
Northern Pintail	Common transient and winter visitor, irregular summer visitor; lakes, ponds, and streams.
Blue-winged Teal	Fairly common transient, rare to uncommon winter visitor; ponds. One nesting record: May 10, 1983 {pair with 6 young}, s.w. Phoenix [RB].
Cinnamon Teal	Uncommon summer resident and winter visitor, common transient (locally abundant in fall); ponds, streams, and canals.
Northern Shoveler	Common transient, common (locally abundant) winter visitor, irregular summer visitor in small numbers; lakes, ponds, and streams.
Gadwall	Common transient and winter visitor, rare summer visitor; lakes, ponds, and streams.
Eurasian Wigeon	Rare but regular winter visitor in very small numbers; ponds and streams.
American Wigeon	Fairly common transient, common (locally abundant) winter visitor, rare summer visitor; lakes, ponds, and streams.
Canvasback	Uncommon transient and winter visitor; lakes and ponds.
Redhead	Fairly common transient and winter visitor, irregular summer visitor in small numbers; lakes and ponds. One nesting record: May 30, 1993 {pair with 9 young}, Rio Verde [AV].
Ring-necked Duck	Common transient and winter visitor; lakes and ponds.

Braces, { }, denote number of individuals, etc.   **Brackets, [ ], denote observers or institutions**

Tufted Duck – Ruddy Duck

Species	Nest	Jan.	Feb.	Mar.	Apr.	May	June	July	Aug.	Sept.	Oct.	Nov.	Dec.
Tufted Duck		~~~	~~~	~~								~~	~~~
Greater Scaup		····	····	····	····	·						····	····
Lesser Scaup		----	----	----	----	----	----	----	----	----	▬	----	----
Oldsquaw		····	····	····	····	····	····				·	····	····
Black Scoter												~	
Surf Scoter				·			·				····	····	·
White-winged Scoter		----	----	----	----	----	----	----	----	----	----	~	~
Common Goldeneye		----	----	----	·	----	----	----	----	----	----	----	----
Barrow's Goldeneye			·	·									
Bufflehead		····	····	····	····	····	····			····	····		
Hooded Merganser		----	----	----	----	~	----	----	----	----	----	----	----
Common Merganser		▬	▬	▬	▬	▬	·	·	▬	▬	▬	▬	▬
Red-breasted Merganser		----	----	----	----	·	·	·	----	----	----	----	----
Ruddy Duck	N	----	----	----	▬	▬	----	----	----	----	▬	----	----

Legend:

▬▬▬ Abundant	Common	Uncom. or Irreg.	Accidental
▪▪▪▪ Irreg. Abund.	—— Fairly Com.	········ Rare or Casual	~~~ Ind. Extended Stay

- 72 -

Tufted Duck – Ruddy Duck

Tufted Duck Accidental. Jan. 8 – Mar. 31, 1993 and Nov. 13 – Dec. 18, 1993 {♂}. Red Mountain Ranch, Mesa [*fide* SG, m.ob., photos TG, RJo]. Feb. 27 – Mar. 29, 1995 {♂}. Greenfield Park and Red Mountain Ranch, Mesa [*fide* SG].

Greater Scaup Rare winter visitor; lakes and ponds.

Lesser Scaup Fairly common transient and winter visitor, rare irregular summer visitor; lakes and ponds.

Oldsquaw Casual winter visitor; lakes and ponds.

Black Scoter Accidental. Nov. 4, 1975 {2}, Nov. 5–12, 1975 {3}, 35th Ave. ponds, s. w. Phoenix [SD, HL *et al.*, photo JW].

Surf Scoter Rare transient; lakes and ponds.

White-winged Scoter Accidental. Oct. 28 – Nov. 3, 1970 {1 – 2}, 35th Ave. ponds, s.w. Phoenix [BB, SD *et al.*]. Oct. 31 – Nov. 12, 1971 {2 –1}, 35th Ave. ponds [SF, BB *et al.*]. Dec. 6–10, 1990 {1} Chandler ponds [HW *et al.*].

Common Goldeneye Uncommon winter visitor; lakes, ponds, and streams.

Barrow's Goldeneye Accidental. Mar. 2, 1982 {♂}, 7th Ave. pond, Phoenix [RB].

Bufflehead Fairly common winter visitor; lakes, ponds, and streams.

Hooded Merganser Uncommon winter visitor; lakes, ponds, and streams.

Common Merganser Common winter visitor (sometimes in large numbers); lakes and Salt and Verde Rivers. Uncommon transient; lakes, ponds, and streams.

Red-breasted Merganser Uncommon winter visitor, casual summer visitor; lakes, ponds, and streams.

Ruddy Duck Uncommon summer resident, common (locally abundant) winter visitor; lakes and ponds.

Braces, {}, denote number of individuals, etc.   Brackets, [], denote observers or institutions

Black Vulture – Harris' Hawk

Species	Nest	Jan.	Feb.	Mar.	Apr.	May	June	July	Aug.	Sept.	Oct.	Nov.	Dec.
Black Vulture													
Turkey Vulture	N												
Osprey	NF												
White-tailed Kite	N												
Mississippi Kite	N-1												
Bald Eagle	N												
Northern Harrier													
Sharp-shinned Hawk													
Cooper's Hawk	N												
Northern Goshawk													
Common Black-Hawk	N												
Harris' Hawk	N												

Legend:

Abundant	Common	Uncom. or Irreg.
Irreg. Abund.	Fairly Com.	Rare or Casual
	· · · Accidental	~~~ Ind. Extended Stay

Black Vulture – Harris' Hawk

Black Vulture Rare local visitor; southwest Phoenix. Evidence of possible nesting in the Sierra Estrella Mts. [LS, DB].

Turkey Vulture Common summer resident, common to abundant transient; generally distributed. Uncommon local winter visitor in western part of county.

Osprey Fairly common transient and winter visitor, uncommon summer visitor; lakes and streams. Nested near Granite Reef Dam before 1951. Present during nesting season on Salt, Verde, and Gila Rivers.

White-tailed Kite Uncommon late fall and winter visitor; rare and irregular spring, summer, and early fall visitor; farm fields. A courting pair June 9, 1986, s.e.of Buckeye suggested breeding [CH]. Nested at Robbins Butte {pair with two young} June 16, 1993 [JB].

Mississippi Kite Casual spring and summer visitor; riparian areas. One nesting record: June 1976 {pair with 1 young}, Verde River [RG].

Bald Eagle Uncommon resident; lakes and rivers. Currently eight pairs of breeding adults. Juveniles and most sub-adults migrate north as far as Canada in summer and return in Sept./Oct. [GB]. Migrant birds from northern populations increase numbers in some winters.

Northern Harrier Common transient and winter visitor; fields, marshes, and open scrub deserts.

Sharp-shinned Hawk Uncommon transient, fairly common winter visitor; generally distributed.

Cooper's Hawk Uncommon summer resident; riparian areas. Fairly common transient and winter visitor; generally distributed.

Northern Goshawk Rare winter visitor; generally distributed.

Common Black-Hawk Rare transient and uncommon local summer resident; riparian areas in Sonoran Zones.

Harris' Hawk Common local resident; riparian areas, Lower Sonoran Desert, and suburban areas.

Braces, { }, denote number of individuals, etc.   Brackets, [ ], denote observers or institutions

75

Gray Hawk – Prairie Falcon

Species	Nest	Jan.	Feb.	Mar.	Apr.	May	June	July	Aug.	Sept.	Oct.	Nov.	Dec.
Gray Hawk	N-1												
Red-shouldered Hawk													
Broad-winged Hawk													
Swainson's Hawk													
White-tailed Hawk													
Zone-tailed Hawk	N												
Red-tailed Hawk	N												
Ferruginous Hawk	N												
Rough-legged Hawk													
Golden Eagle	N												
Crested Caracara													
American Kestrel	N												
Merlin													
Prairie Falcon	N												

Legend:

Abundant	Common	Uncom. or Irreg.	Accidental
Irreg. Abund.	Fairly Com.	Rare or Casual	Ind. Extended Stay

Gray Hawk – Prairie Falcon

Gray Hawk	Casual visitor; riparian areas in Sonoran Zones. One nesting record: June 9, 1963 {pair at a nest}, near Seven Springs [CS].
Red-shouldered Hawk	Casual winter visitor to lowland riparian areas.
Broad-winged Hawk	Accidental. Mar. 16, 1975 {1}, Verde River, e. of Phoenix [ST, SM]. Dec. 18, 1976 {imm. Broad-winged or Gray} s.w. Phoenix [DSz *et al.*]. Feb. 13, 1992 {imm.}, below Bartlett Dam [LA, JR, LC, ME].
Swainson's Hawk	Fairly common spring transient, common fall transient, often in flocks; fields and desert.
White-tailed Hawk	Accidental. Three records during December and January, 1954-55, in n.w. Phoenix and w. of Gila Bend [RJ, AM, LD, VH].
Zone-tailed Hawk	Uncommon local summer resident; riparian areas of Upper Sonoran Zone and locally at higher elevations. Casual winter visitor to lowlands.
Red-tailed Hawk	Common resident, additional visitors in winter; generally distributed.
Ferruginous Hawk	Fairly common transient and winter visitor; fields.
Rough-legged Hawk	Rare winter visitor; fields.
Golden Eagle	Rare resident; Upper Sonoran and Transition Zones. Casual in Lower Sonoran Zone.
Crested Caracara	Casual visitor to lowlands.
American Kestrel	Fairly common summer resident, common transient, and winter visitor; generally distributed.
Merlin	Rare winter visitor; generally distributed.
Prairie Falcon	Rare local resident on cliffs in the Phoenix area and n. of Phoenix. Uncommon transient and winter visitor; generally distributed, with a few wintering on the tops of tall urban buildings.

Braces, { }, denote number of individuals, etc.   Brackets, [ ], denote observers or institutions

Peregrine Falcon – Mountain Plover

Species	Nest	Jan.	Feb.	Mar.	Apr.	May	June	July	Aug.	Sept.	Oct.	Nov.	Dec.
Peregrine Falcon	N												
Wild Turkey	N												
Gambel's Quail	N												
Clapper Rail	N												
Virginia Rail	N												
Sora	NF												
Common Moorhen	N												
American Coot	N												
Sandhill Crane													
Black-bellied Plover													
American Golden-Plover													
Snowy Plover	N												
Semipalmated Plover													
Killdeer	N												
Mountain Plover													

Legend:

Abundant	Common	Uncom. or Irreg.	Accidental
Irreg. Abund.	Fairly Com.	Rare or Casual	Ind. Extended Stay

- 78 -

Peregrine Falcon – Mountain Plover

Peregrine Falcon	Rare local resident on cliffs near Salt River reservoirs. Uncommon transient and winter visitor; generally distributed, with a few wintering on the tops of tall urban buildings.
Wild Turkey	Rare resident in Transition Zone forests on Four Peaks.
Gambel's Quail	Common resident, sometimes in large numbers; Lower and Upper Sonoran Zones.
Clapper Rail	Rare local summer resident, some remaining over winter; cattail marshes in Salt and Gila Rivers, south and west of Phoenix.
Virginia Rail	Rare local summer resident, fairly common local winter visitor; cattail marshes.
Sora	Fairly common local winter visitor; cattail marshes. None found in former nesting areas since 1975.
Common Moorhen	Fairly common resident; streams, marshes, and ponds.
American Coot	Common summer resident, abundant winter visitor; lakes, ponds, streams, and marshes.
Sandhill Crane	Irregular, rare winter visitor; fields.
Black-bellied Plover	Uncommon fall transient, rare spring transient, one winter record; ponds.
American Golden-Plover	Rare fall and spring transient; ponds.
Snowy Plover	Uncommon transient, two winter records; ponds. Nested at Painted Rock Dam, summers of 1974, 1980, and 1993.
Semipalmated Plover	Fairly common transient, two winter records; ponds.
Killdeer	Common summer resident and winter visitor, abundant transient; ponds, streams, and fields.
Mountain Plover	Rare local winter visitor; barren, fallow fields. Casual fall and spring transient; dry lake and pond edges.

Braces, {}, denote number of individuals, etc.   Brackets, [], denote observers or institutions

Black-necked Stilt – Sanderling

Species	Nest	Jan.	Feb.	Mar.	Apr.	May	June	July	Aug.	Sept.	Oct.	Nov.	Dec.
Black-necked Stilt	N												
American Avocet	N												
Greater Yellowlegs													
Lesser Yellowlegs													
Solitary Sandpiper													
Willet													
Wandering Tattler													
Spotted Sandpiper													
Upland Sandpiper													
Whimbrel													
Long-billed Curlew													
Marbled Godwit													
Ruddy Turnstone													
Red Knot													
Sanderling													

Legend:

Abundant	Common	Uncom. or Irreg.
Irreg. Abund.	Fairly Com.	Rare or Casual
		Accidental · · ·
		Ind. Extended Stay ~~~~

Black-necked Stilt – Sanderling

Black-necked Stilt	Common local summer resident, abundant transient, fairly common winter visitor; ponds and marshes.
American Avocet	Irregular local summer resident, common fall transient, fairly common spring transient, rare winter visitor; lakes, ponds, and marshes.
Greater Yellowlegs	Common transient, fairly common winter visitor; lakes, ponds, streams, and flooded fields.
Lesser Yellowlegs	Fairly common transient, rare winter visitor; lakes, ponds, streams, and flooded fields.
Solitary Sandpiper	Uncommon transient, casual winter visitor; ponds and streams.
Willet	Uncommon transient, a few summer records; ponds and flooded fields.
Wandering Tattler	Accidental. Sept. 18 – Oct. 9, 1971 {1}, 35th Ave. ponds, Phoenix [BB *et al.*, photo RW]. Call notes and field marks ruled out Gray-tailed Tattler [Witzeman, R. 1972. *California Birds* 3: 13–15].
Spotted Sandpiper	Common transient and winter visitor, a few summer records; lakes, ponds, streams, and canals.
Upland Sandpiper	Accidental. Oct. 17–18, 1961 {3}, Mesa [CR, SD *et al.*]. Oct. 5, 1974 {1}, Riggs Rd. ponds, s. of Chandler [ST, S & KM].
Whimbrel	Casual transient; ponds.
Long-billed Curlew	Common spring transient, fairly common fall transient, uncommon winter visitor; fields and ponds in south and west part of county.
Marbled Godwit	Uncommon transient; ponds and flooded fields.
Ruddy Turnstone	Casual fall transient; ponds.
Red Knot	Casual fall transient; ponds.
Sanderling	Uncommon fall transient, casual spring transient, four winter records; ponds.

Braces, {}, denote number of individuals, etc.   Brackets, [], denote observers or institutions

Semipalmated Sandpiper – Red-necked Phalarope

Species	Nest	Jan.	Feb.	Mar.	Apr.	May	June	July	Aug.	Sept.	Oct.	Nov.	Dec.
Semipalmated Sandpiper													
Western Sandpiper													
Least Sandpiper													
Baird's Sandpiper													
Pectoral Sandpiper													
Sharp-tailed Sandpiper													
Dunlin													
Stilt Sandpiper													
Ruff													
Short-billed Dowitcher													
Long-billed Dowitcher													
Common Snipe													
Wilson's Phalarope													
Red-necked Phalarope													

Legend:

Symbol	Meaning
▇	Abundant
▮▮▮	Irreg. Abund.
—	Common
—	Fairly Com.
- - - -	Uncom. or Irreg.
· · · · ·	Rare or Casual
•	Accidental
~~	Ind. Extended Stay

Semipalmated Sandpiper – Red-necked Phalarope	
Semipalmated Sandpiper	Uncommon fall transient, rare spring transient; ponds.
Western Sandpiper	Common to abundant fall transient, common spring transient, rare to uncommon winter visitor; ponds and streams.
Least Sandpiper	Abundant transient and winter visitor; ponds and streams.
Baird's Sandpiper	Fairly common fall transient, rare spring transient; ponds.
Pectoral Sandpiper	Fairly common fall transient, no documented winter records; ponds.
Sharp-tailed Sandpiper	Accidental. Oct. 15–18, 1972 {1}, Riggs Rd. ponds, s. of Chandler [photo RW *et al.*]. Oct. 11, 1985 {1}, 83rd Ave. ponds, s.w. Phoenix [DS *et al.*].
Dunlin	Uncommon transient and winter visitor; ponds.
Stilt Sandpiper	Uncommon fall transient, rare spring transient; ponds.
Ruff	Accidental. Nov. 10, 1974 – Feb. 17, 1975 {1}, 35th Ave. ponds, Phoenix [RN, DD *et al.*, photos JW, RW]. Oct. 11–20, 1985 {1}, 83rd Ave. ponds, s.w. Phoenix [DS *et al.*].
Short-billed Dowitcher	Uncommon fall transient, rare spring transient; ponds.
Long-billed Dowitcher	Common transient and winter visitor; ponds and streams.
Common Snipe	Common winter visitor; ponds, marshes, streams, and wet fields.
Wilson's Phalarope	Common to abundant transient (often in large numbers), two winter records; lakes and ponds.
Red-necked Phalarope	Fairly common fall transient, rare spring transient; lakes and ponds.
Braces, { }, denote number of individuals, etc.	Brackets, [ ], denote observers or institutions

Red Phalarope – Sabine's Gull

Species	Nest	Jan.	Feb.	Mar.	Apr.	May	June	July	Aug.	Sept.	Oct.	Nov.	Dec.
Red Phalarope		•				•			•	....	....	....	
Pomarine Jaeger							~						
Parasitic Jaeger									•	•			
Long-tailed Jaeger										~			
Laughing Gull									~~~~	~~~~			
Franklin's Gull				•				....					
Bonaparte's Gull		....		------	------	------	------	------	------	------	------		
Heermann's Gull					•					•	•	•	
Ring-billed Gull					•	•							
California Gull		------	•	•	------								
Herring Gull		....	....	•				•			....	....	....
Western Gull												•	
Glaucous Gull									~		~~~~	~~~~	~
Black-legged Kittiwake												~~~~	
Sabine's Gull										....	....		....

Abundant ▬▬	**Common** ▬▬	**Uncom. or Irreg.** ------	**Accidental** • •
Irreg. Abund. ▪▪▪▪	**Fairly Com.** ▬	**Rare or Casual**	**Ind. Extended Stay** ~~~~

- 84 -

Red Phalarope – Sabine's Gull

Red Phalarope	Rare fall transient, one winter record; lakes and ponds.
Pomarine Jaeger	Accidental. June 7–10, 1985 {adult}, Lake Pleasant [CBe *et al.*].
Parasitic Jaeger	Accidental. Aug. 23, 1980 {1}, Painted Rock Dam [RB, RF, CK]. Sept. 1, 1984 {juv. specimen} n. of Gila Bend [*fide* DT, KK].
Long-tailed Jaeger	Accidental. Sept. 7–21, 1970 {juv.} 35th Ave. ponds, Phoenix [photos RW, m.ob, iden. by KK].
Laughing Gull	Accidental. Aug. 2 – Sept. 30, 1993 {1 – 2 adults}, Painted Rock Darr [BT, GMc, m.ob, photo RW].
Franklin's Gull	Uncommon transient; lakes and ponds.
Bonaparte's Gull	Uncommon transient, rare winter visitor; lakes and ponds.
Heermann's Gull	Casual fall visitor, one spring record; lakes and ponds.
Ring-billed Gull	Fairly common visitor; lakes, ponds, and streams.
California Gull	Uncommon transient and winter visitor, a few summer records; lakes and ponds.
Herring Gull	Casual transient and winter visitor; lakes and ponds.
Western Gull	Accidental. Nov. 6, 1963 {1}, Nov. 8, 1963 {found dead}, 35th Ave. ponds [MB, SD]. July 18,1979 {large dark-backed adult – either this species or Yellow-footed Gull}, Painted Rock Dam [DSz].
Glaucous Gull	Accidental. Nov. 17 – Dec. 4, 1988 {first year}, Indian Bend Wash Park pond, Scottsdale [BK, m.ob, photos TG, GR]. Dec. 24, 1993 – Jan. 1, 1994 {first year}, Painted Rock Dam [photo CB *et al.*].
Black-legged Kittiwake	Casual late fall and early winter transient, one spring record; lakes and ponds.
Sabine's Gull	Rare fall transient; lakes and ponds.

Braces, { }, denote number of individuals, etc.	Brackets, [ ], denote observers or institutions

Caspian Tern – Ruddy Ground-Dove

Species	Nest	Jan.	Feb.	Mar.	Apr.	May	June	July	Aug.	Sept.	Oct.	Nov.	Dec.
Caspian Tern													
Elegant Tern													
Common Tern													
Forster's Tern													
Least Tern													
Black Tern													
Black Skimmer													
Rock Dove	N												
Band-tailed Pigeon	N												
White-winged Dove	N												
Mourning Dove	N												
Inca Dove	N												
Common Ground-Dove	N												
Ruddy Ground-Dove	N												

Legend:

▬▬ Abundant	── Common	------ Uncom. or Irreg.
▪▪▪▪ Irreg. Abund.	── Fairly Com.	·········· Rare or Casual
		· Accidental
		∼∼∼ Ind. Extended Stay

- 86 -

Caspian Tern – Ruddy Ground-Dove

Caspian Tern	Uncommon transient; lakes and ponds.
Elegant Tern	Accidental. May 30, 1988 {1}, Painted Rock Dam [RF *et al.*, photo DS].
Common Tern	Uncommon fall transient; lakes and ponds.
Forster's Tern	Fairly common transient, two winter records; lakes and ponds.
Least Tern	Casual spring, summer, and early fall transient; lakes and ponds.
Black Tern	Uncommon fall transient, rare spring transient; lakes and ponds.
Black Skimmer	Accidental. July 14, 1993 {1}, Painted Rock Dam [GR *et al.*].
Rock Dove	Abundant resident; suburban and agricultural areas.
Band-tailed Pigeon	Uncommon local summer resident in Transition Zone forests. Casual wanderer to lower elevations, including four winter records.
White-winged Dove	Abundant summer resident, uncommon to rare winterer; Sonoran Zones.
Mourning Dove	Abundant resident, with increased numbers in fall and winter; generally distributed, but mainly in agricultural and suburban areas.
Inca Dove	Abundant resident; suburban areas, farmyards, and fields.
Common Ground-Dove	Fairly common summer resident, uncommon winter resident; fields and hedgerows.
Ruddy Ground-Dove	Casual fall and winter visitor; fields, riparian areas, and pond edges. One nesting record: May 15, 1993 {pair with one young}, Hassayampa River Preserve, Wickenburg [JH].

Braces, {}, denote number of individuals, etc.　　　　Brackets, [], denote observers or institutions

Yellow-billed Cuckoo – Northern Saw-whet Owl

Species	Nest	Jan.	Feb.	Mar.	Apr.	May	June	July	Aug.	Sept.	Oct.	Nov.	Dec.
Yellow-billed Cuckoo	N					•	-----	-----	•	•	•	•	
Greater Roadrunner	N							•	•	•	•	•	•
Groove-billed Ani			~~~~	~~~~									
Barn Owl	N	-----	-----	-----	-----	-----	-----	-----	-----	-----	-----	-----	-----
Flammulated Owl	N		•		-----			....	-----	....	....	•	-----	
Western Screech-Owl	N												
Great Horned Owl	N												
Northern Pygmy-Owl	N	-----											-----
Ferruginous Pygmy-Owl	NF												
Elf Owl	N									••			•
Burrowing Owl	N	....	....	....	....	....	....	....	....	....	....	....	....
Spotted Owl	N	....	....	....	....	....	....	....	....	....	....	....	....
Long-eared Owl	N	....	....	....	....	....	....	....	....	....	....	....	....
Short-eared Owl		-----	-----	-----							-----	-----	-----
Northern Saw-whet Owl	N	....	....	....	....	....	....	....	....	....	....	....	....

Legend:

▬▬ Abundant	----- Uncom. or Irreg.
▪▪▪ Irreg. Abund.	.... Rare or Casual
▬ Common	• Accidental
— Fairly Com.	~~~ Ind. Extended Stay

- 88 -

Yellow-billed Cuckoo – Northern Saw-whet Owl

Yellow-billed Cuckoo	Uncommon local summer resident; riparian areas of Lower Sonoran Zone.
Greater Roadrunner	Common resident; desert, agricultural, and suburban areas.
Groove-billed Ani	Casual visitor; riparian and brushy areas.
Barn Owl	Uncommon local resident; fields, farmyards, suburban palm trees, and under some bridges.
Flammulated Owl	Uncommon summer resident in Transition Zone forests. Casual fall transient at lower elevations.
Western Screech-Owl	Common resident; riparian woodlands, Sonoran Desert, and suburban areas.
Great Horned Owl	Common resident; riparian woodlands, Sonoran Desert, and suburban areas.
Northern Pygmy-Owl	Uncommon local resident in Transition Zone forests.
Ferruginous Pygmy-Owl	Resident near confluence of Salt and Gila Rivers, at New River. and near Agua Caliente in late 1800's and early 1900's. Until 1951, a casual resident near confluence of Salt and Verde Rivers. One heard at Blue Point cottonwoods in May 1971 [R.J].
Elf Owl	Fairly common local summer resident, one December specimen record; Sonoran and Transition Zones.
Burrowing Owl	Uncommon local resident; fields and Lower Sonoran Desert.
Spotted Owl	Rare local resident; Superstition Wilderness Area and Mazatzal Mountains.
Long-eared Owl	Rare local resident; Sonoran Zones. Rare winter visitor; Lower Sonoran Desert.
Short-eared Owl	Uncommon local winter visitor; cultivated fields, s.w. Phoenix.
Northern Saw-whet Owl	Rare resident in Transition Zone forests. Casual in fall and winter at lower elevations.

Braces, {}, denote number of individuals, etc.   Brackets, [], denote observers or institutions

Lesser Nighthawk – Broad-tailed Hummingbird

Species	Nest	Jan.	Feb.	Mar.	Apr.	May	June	July	Aug.	Sept.	Oct.	Nov.	Dec.
Lesser Nighthawk	N												
Common Nighthawk													
Common Poorwill	N												
Whip-poor-will	N												
Chimney Swift													
Vaux's Swift													
White-throated Swift	N												
Broad-billed Hummingbird	N-1												
Magnificent Hummingbird													
Plain-capped Starthroat													
Black-chinned Hummingbird	N												
Anna's Hummingbird	N												
Costa's Hummingbird	N												
Calliope Hummingbird													
Broad-tailed Hummingbird	N												

Legend:

Abundant	Common
Irreg. Abund.	Fairly Com.
------- Uncom. or Irreg.	• Accidental
.... Rare or Casual	~~~ Ind. Extended Stay

Lesser Nighthawk – Broad-tailed Hummingbird

Species	Status
Lesser Nighthawk	Common summer resident, rare winter visitor; Lower Sonoran Zone.
Common Nighthawk	Rare fall transient in low elevation areas.
Common Poorwill	Fairly common summer resident. Winter status unclear; at least some remain and hibernate. Sonoran Zones.
Whip-poor-will	Rare summer resident in Mazatzal and Superstition Mountains. Scattered records at lower elevations.
Chimney Swift	Casual transient in lowlands.
Vaux's Swift	Uncommon transient; generally distributed.
White-throated Swift	Uncommon resident, fairly common transient and winter visitor; lakes, streams, cliffs, fields, and tall urban buildings.
Broad-billed Hummingbird	Rare visitor; residential feeders and riparian areas. One nesting record, April 18, 1980 {nest with young}, n.e. Phoenix [fide KI].
Magnificent Hummingbird	Casual transient.
Plain-capped Starthroat	Accidental. Oct. 17 - Nov. 28, 1978 {1}, n. Phoenix [JY, m.ob., photos GMe].
Black-chinned Hummingbird	Common summer resident; suburban and riparian areas in Sonoran Zones.
Anna's Hummingbird	Common resident, especially in fall and winter; suburban areas, riparian areas, and fields in Sonoran Zones. Rare in Transition Zone in spring and summer.
Costa's Hummingbird	Fairly common winter and spring resident, rare in summer and early fall; Sonoran Zones.
Calliope Hummingbird	Casual transient, mainly in higher elevations. Two spring records at lower elevations in Phoenix.
Broad-tailed Hummingbird	Fairly common summer resident in Transition Zone forests. Uncommon to rare transient at lower elevations, mainly in spring.

Braces, { }, denote number of individuals, etc.   Brackets, [ ], denote observers or institutions

Rufous Hummingbird – Gilded Flicker

Species	Nest	Jan.	Feb.	Mar.	Apr.	May	June	July	Aug.	Sept.	Oct.	Nov.	Dec.
Rufous Hummingbird													
Elegant Trogon													
Belted Kingfisher	NF												
Lewis' Woodpecker													
Red-headed Woodpecker	N												
Acorn Woodpecker	N												
Gila Woodpecker	N												
Yellow-bellied Sapsucker													
Red-naped Sapsucker													
Red-breasted Sapsucker													
Williamson's Sapsucker	N												
Ladder-backed Woodpecker	N												
Downy Woodpecker	N												
Hairy Woodpecker	N												
Northern Flicker	N												
"Red-shafted"	N												
"Yellow-shafted"													
Gilded Flicker	N												

Legend:

▬▬ Abundant	■■■ Irreg. Abund.
Common	------ Uncom. or Irreg.
—— Fairly Com.	·········· Rare or Casual
· Accidental	∼∼∼ Ind. Extended Stay

Rufous Hummingbird – Gilded Flicker

Rufous Hummingbird	Common fall transient, uncommon spring transient; suburban and riparian areas.
Elegant Trogon	Accidental. Late June 1989 {1}, n. of Carefree [CTh, *fide* ER, photo LO].
Belted Kingfisher	Fairly common winter visitor; ponds, streams, and canals. Nested along Gila River near Komatke before 1928 [*fide* AR].
Lewis' Woodpecker	Irregular winter visitor in moist lowlands; pecan groves, cemeteries, golf courses, and suburban yards.
Red-headed Woodpecker	Accidental. March – May, 1959 {1}, Phoenix yard [DFe, H&RC, SD *et al*].
Acorn Woodpecker	Rare resident in Transition Zone oaks. Irregular fall and winter wanderer to lower elevations.
Gila Woodpecker	Common resident; Lower Sonoran Zone.
Yellow-bellied Sapsucker	Casual fall, winter, and spring visitor; Sonoran Zones.
Red-naped Sapsucker	Fairly common fall transient and winter visitor; Sonoran Zones.
Red-breasted Sapsucker	Casual fall and winter visitor; Sonoran Zones.
Williamson's Sapsucker	Rare transient and winter visitor; Sonoran and Transition Zones.
Ladder-backed Woodpecker	Fairly common resident; riparian and desert areas in Lower Sonoran Zone, and ranging into lower Upper Sonoran Zone.
Downy Woodpecker	Accidental. Jan. 2–15, 1976 {1}, s.w. Phoenix [RB *et al*].
Hairy Woodpecker	Uncommon resident in Transition Zone forests. Rare winter wanderer to lower elevations.
Northern Flicker	
"*Red-shafted*"	Uncommon summer resident in Transition Zone forests. Common winter visitor in lowlands.
"*Yellow-shafted*"	Rare transient and winter visitor in lowlands.
Gilded Flicker	Fairly common resident; desert and riparian areas in Lower Sonoran Zone.

Braces, {}, denote number of individuals, etc.   Brackets, [], denote observers or institutions

Northern Beardless-Tyrannulet – Black Phoebe

Species	Nest	Jan.	Feb.	Mar.	Apr.	May	June	July	Aug.	Sept.	Oct.	Nov.	Dec.
Northern Beardless-Tyrannulet													
Olive-sided Flycatcher													
Greater Pewee													
Western Wood-Pewee	N												
Willow Flycatcher													
Least Flycatcher													
Hammond's Flycatcher													
Dusky Flycatcher													
Gray Flycatcher													
Pacific-slope Flycatcher													
Cordilleran Flycatcher													
Black Phoebe	N												

Legend:

▬▬ Abundant	▬▬ Common	· · Accidental
▪▪▪ Irreg. Abund.	— Fairly Com.	~~~ Ind. Extended Stay
	------ Uncom. or Irreg.	
	.... Rare or Casual	

- 94 -

Northern Beardless-Tyrannulet – Black Phoebe

Northern Beardless-Tyrannulet	Accidental. June 4, 1975 {1}, Verde River, Ft. McDowell Indian Reservation [ST].
Olive-sided Flycatcher	Uncommon transient; generally distributed.
Greater Pewee	Uncommon transient in Transition Zone forests. Casual winter visitor to lowlands.
Western Wood-Pewee	Common summer resident; riparian areas, Upper Sonoran and Transition Zones. Common widespread transient; wooded habitats, including suburban areas.
Willow Flycatcher	Uncommon transient; generally distributed. A few historical summer records.
Least Flycatcher	Accidental. Apr. 12, 1978 {1}, 91st Ave. & Salt River, Phoenix; specimen [REA]. Dec. 22–24, 1986 {1}, Salt River, e. of Phoenix [RN, DS].
Hammond's Flycatcher	Common fall transient, fairly common spring transient, rare winter visitor; riparian and suburban areas. Exact time of migration for this and following species not fully determined due to difficulty in identification.
Dusky Flycatcher	Common fall transient, fairly common spring transient; generally distributed. Rare winter visitor; riparian and suburban areas.
Gray Flycatcher	Fairly common transient and winter visitor; riparian areas, hedgerows, and mesquite trees.
Pacific-slope Flycatcher	Common transient (i.e. 'western' type flycatchers are common in migration in the lowlands and this species is expected more in the lowlands on migration than the following species). A few winter records, plus some winter records of 'western' type not identified to species; lowlands.
Cordilleran Flycatcher	Uncommon transient; small numbers in lowlands, expected more at higher elevations.
Black Phoebe	Common resident; streams and ponds. Influx of additional numbers from higher elevations during migration and winter when it can be found near any body of water.

Braces, { }, denote number of individuals, etc.	Brackets, [ ], denote observers or institutions

Eastern Phoebe – Horned Lark

Species	Nest	Jan.	Feb.	Mar.	Apr.	May	June	July	Aug.	Sept.	Oct.	Nov.	Dec.
Eastern Phoebe		· · · · · · · · ·	· · · · · · · · ·	· · · · · · · · ·	· · · · · · ·					· · · · · · ·	· · · · · · · · ·	· ·	· · · · · · · ·
Say's Phoebe	N												
Vermilion Flycatcher	N												
Dusky-capped Flycatcher						·							
Ash-throated Flycatcher	N												
Brown-crested Flycatcher	N												
Sulphur-bellied Flycatcher								·					
Tropical Kingbird						· ·							
Cassin's Kingbird	N												
Western Kingbird	N												
Eastern Kingbird										· ·			
Scissor-tailed Flycatcher										·	·		
Horned Lark	N												

Abundant ▬▬▬	Common ▬▬▬	Uncom. or Irreg. − − −	Accidental · ·
Irreg. Abund. ▪▪▪▪	Fairly Com. ▬▬	Rare or Casual · · · · ·	Ind. Extended Stay ∼∼∼

Eastern Phoebe – Horned Lark

Eastern Phoebe	Rare transient and winter visitor; riparian and suburban areas.
Say's Phoebe	Fairly common summer resident, common winter visitor; suburban areas and open country in Lower and Upper Sonoran Zones. Some post-breeding migration out of these areas during July and August.
Vermilion Flycatcher	Fairly common local resident; riparian and agricultural areas.
Dusky-capped Flycatcher	Accidental. May 30, 1976 {1}, Superstition Mts. [RN, CB *et al.*]. May 11, 1980 {1}, Tempe [ST].
Ash-throated Flycatcher	Common summer resident, uncommon winter visitor; riparian areas and Lower Sonoran Desert, especially in mesquite habitat; Upper Sonoran pinyon/juniper habitat.
Brown-crested Flycatcher	Common summer resident; Lower Sonoran Desert, riparian and suburban areas.
Sulphur-bellied Flycatcher	Accidental. July 28, 1990 {1}, Slate Creek Divide [DP *et al.*]. July 2, 1992 {imm.}, Lower Camp Creek [SD, LH, HL].
Tropical Kingbird	Accidental. May 16, 1951 {1}, Phoenix [JK, *B. of A.*]. May 19, 1956 (building nest), Phoenix; specimen [JSW]. May 30, 1975 {1}, Granite Reef Campground [ST].
Cassin's Kingbird	Fairly common summer resident; most Upper Sonoran Zone habitats, especially wooded streamsides, and up to Transition Zone pines. Uncommon transient; generally distributed.
Western Kingbird	Common spring transient and summer resident, abundant fall transient, no documented winter records; Lower Sonoran Zone and some Upper Sonoran Zone habitats.
Eastern Kingbird	Accidental. Sept. 8, 1991 {1}, s.w. Phoenix [MJ, TG]. Sept. 6, 1994 {1}, Paloma [KRa].
Scissor-tailed Flycatcher	Casual spring, summer and fall visitor; lowlands.
Horned Lark	Abundant winter visitor, fairly common summer resident; barren and plowed fields; flat, open deserts and pastures.
Braces, { }, denote number of individuals, etc.	Brackets, [ ], denote observers or institutions

Purple Martin – Mexican Jay

Species	Nest	Jan.	Feb.	Mar.	Apr.	May	June	July	Aug.	Sept.	Oct.	Nov.	Dec.
Purple Martin	N-1												
Tree Swallow													
Violet-green Swallow	N												
Northern Rough-winged Swallow	N												
Bank Swallow													
Cliff Swallow	N												
Cave Swallow													
Barn Swallow	N-1												
Steller's Jay	N												
Western Scrub-Jay	N												
Mexican Jay													

Legend:

▬ Abundant	▬ ▬ Irreg. Abund.
─── Common	─── Fairly Com.
-------- Uncom. or Irreg.	········ Rare or Casual
· Accidental	～～～ Ind. Extended Stay

Purple Martin – Mexican Jay

Purple Martin Rare spring and fall transient, rare summer visitor; lowlands. One nesting record: Sept. 30, 1995 [adults feeding 1 young in air], Sand Tank Mts., s.e. of Gila Bend [DG, PH].

Tree Swallow Common transient (sometimes as early as late January/early February), rare winter visitor; streams, ponds, and lakes.

Violet-green Swallow Fairly common summer resident; riparian areas, Upper Sonoran and Transition Zones. Common transient, casual winter visitor; streams, ponds, and lakes.

Northern Rough-winged Swallow Common summer resident; banks of streams and canals. Common transient, uncommon winter visitor; streams, ponds, and lakes.

Bank Swallow Uncommon spring transient, fairly common fall transient, a few winter records; streams, ponds, and lakes.

Cliff Swallow Common summer resident; lakeside, cliffs, and canals; nesting under nearby bridges, on nearby buildings, and other overhangs. Abundant transient, a few winter records; streams, ponds, and lakes.

Cave Swallow Accidental. Dec. 21-31, 1987 {1}, Phon D. Sutton campground, Salt River [TG, MJ, RM, photo HM].

Barn Swallow Uncommon spring transient, common to abundant fall transient, a few December records; streams, ponds, lakes, and agricultural areas. Found nesting at Gilbert sewage ponds, July 1987 [DS, RF].

Steller's Jay Fairly common resident in Transition Zone forests. Irregular winter visitor to lowlands.

Western Scrub-Jay Fairly common resident in Upper Sonoran Zone. Irregular visitor to lowlands.

Mexican Jay Irregular wanderer to higher and mid-elevations in n. e. part of county.

Braces, {}, denote number of individuals, etc.   Brackets, [], denote observers or institutions

Pinyon Jay – Cactus Wren

Species	Nest	Jan.	Feb.	Mar.	Apr.	May	June	July	Aug.	Sept.	Oct.	Nov.	Dec.
Pinyon Jay						·							
Clark's Nutcracker										·	·		
American Crow									·	·	·	·	
Common Raven	N												
Mountain Chickadee	N												
Bridled Titmouse	N												
Plain Titmouse	N												
Verdin	N												
Bushtit	N												
Red-breasted Nuthatch	N												
White-breasted Nuthatch	N												
Pygmy Nuthatch	N												
Brown Creeper	N												
Cactus Wren	N												

Abundant ▬▬	Common ▬▬	Uncom. or Irreg. ------	Accidental ·
Irreg. Abund. ▪▪▪▪	Fairly Com. ▬	Rare or Casual ········	Ind. Extended Stay ~~~

- 100 -

Pinyon Jay – Cactus Wren

Pinyon Jay	Casual fall wanderer, one spring record.
Clark's Nutcracker	Casual wanderer into Transition Zone forests. Two lowland records.
American Crow	Rare transient and winter visitor; streams, ponds, agricultural areas, dumps, and suburban areas. Two summer records on Verde River.
Common Raven	Fairly common summer resident; Upper Sonoran Zone. Common winter visitor; generally distributed, but scarcer in southwest part of county.
Mountain Chickadee	Fairly common resident in Transition Zone forests. Irregular winter visitor to lowlands.
Bridled Titmouse	Fairly common resident; riparian areas in Upper Sonoran Zone. Irregular winter wanderer to lower elevations.
Plain Titmouse	Uncommon resident in Upper Sonoran Zone, especially in pinyon/juniper habitat.
Verdin	Common resident; Lower and Upper Sonoran Zones.
Bushtit	Fairly common resident in Upper Sonoran Zone. Irregular winter visitor to wooded streamsides in Lower Sonoran Zone.
Red-breasted Nuthatch	Uncommon resident in Transition Zone forests. Uncommon transient in lowlands. Irregular winter visitor to lowlands.
White-breasted Nuthatch	Fairly common resident in Transition Zone forests and Upper Sonoran riparian areas. Uncommon winter visitor to lowlands.
Pygmy Nuthatch	Uncommon resident in Transition Zone forests. Rare winter visitor to lowlands.
Brown Creeper	Uncommon resident in Transition Zone forests. Uncommon transient and winter visitor in lowlands.
Cactus Wren	Common resident in Lower Sonoran Zone, especially in cholla cactus habitat. Uncommon resident in Upper Sonoran mesquite habitat.

Braces, { }, denote number of individuals, etc.	Brackets, [ ], denote observers or institutions

Rock Wren – Townsend's Solitaire

Species	Nest	Jan.	Feb.	Mar.	Apr.	May	June	July	Aug.	Sept.	Oct.	Nov.	Dec.
Rock Wren	N												
Canyon Wren	N												
Bewick's Wren	N												
House Wren													
Winter Wren													
Marsh Wren	N												
American Dipper													
Golden-crowned Kinglet													
Ruby-crowned Kinglet													
Blue-gray Gnatcatcher	N												
Black-tailed Gnatcatcher	N												
Western Bluebird	N												
Mountain Bluebird													
Townsend's Solitaire													

Legend:

Abundant	Common	Uncom. or Irreg.
Irreg. Abund.	Fairly Com.	Rare or Casual
	Accidental ·	Ind. Extended Stay ~~~

Rock Wren – Townsend's Solitaire

Rock Wren	Fairly common resident; rocky embankments, hillsides, and cliffs in Lower and Upper Sonoran Zones. Common winter visitor in Lower Sonoran Desert.
Canyon Wren	Fairly common resident; steep embankments and cliffs. Irregular away from these habitats in fall and winter.
Bewick's Wren	Common resident in woodlands, chaparral, and Upper Sonoran Zone riparian areas. Common transient and winter visitor in Lower Sonoran Zone, especially along wooded riparian areas.
House Wren	Fairly common winter visitor; dense brushy areas.
Winter Wren	Rare fall and winter visitor; Lower and Upper Sonoran Zones.
Marsh Wren	Uncommon summer resident; marshes. Fairly common winter visitor; marshes and dense riparian brush.
American Dipper	Accidental. Found below Roosevelt and Horse Mesa Dams about 1920 and Dec. 1938 to Jan. 1939, respectively [Hargrave, L. 1939. *Condor*, 41: 222]. No recent records.
Golden-crowned Kinglet	Rare and irregular winter visitor, more common in invasion winters; Sonoran and Transition Zones.
Ruby-crowned Kinglet	Common transient and winter visitor; generally distributed.
Blue-gray Gnatcatcher	Fairly common summer resident of chaparral and riparian areas in Upper Sonoran Zone. Uncommon winter visitor in riparian areas of Lower Sonoran Zone.
Black-tailed Gnatcatcher	Fairly common resident in Lower Sonoran and saltbush deserts. Locally common resident in salt cedar and mesquite habitat along Gila River.
Western Bluebird	Rare summer resident in Transition Zone forests. Irregular. sometimes abundant, winter visitor in Sonoran Zones: riparian areas, fields and farmyards, especially in trees with mistletoe.
Mountain Bluebird	Irregular winter visitor; open country.
Townsend's Solitaire	Fairly common winter visitor; Upper Sonoran Zone. Irregular in lowlands.

Braces, { }, denote number of individuals, etc.	**Brackets, [ ], denote observers or institutions**

Swainson's Thrush – Le Conte's Thrasher

Species	Nest	Jan.	Feb.	Mar.	Apr.	May	June	July	Aug.	Sept.	Oct.	Nov.	Dec.
Swainson's Thrush													
Hermit Thrush	N												
Wood Thrush													
Rufous-backed Robin													
American Robin	N												
Varied Thrush													
Gray Catbird													
Northern Mockingbird	N												
Sage Thrasher													
Brown Thrasher													
Bendire's Thrasher	N												
Curve-billed Thrasher	N												
Crissal Thrasher	N												
Le Conte's Thrasher	N												

Legend:

Abundant	Common	Uncom. or Irreg.	Accidental
Irreg. Abund.	Fairly Com.	Rare or Casual	Ind. Extended Stay

Swainson's Thrush – Le Conte's Thrasher

Swainson's Thrush	Uncommon transient; woodlands and suburban areas.
Hermit Thrush	Uncommon summer resident in Transition Zone forests. Fairly common winter visitor in lowland woodlands and suburban areas.
Wood Thrush	Accidental. Oct. 16, 1971 {1}, Phoenix yard [RB,SD].
Rufous-backed Robin	Casual late fall, winter, and spring visitor; riparian and suburban areas.
American Robin	Rare summer suburban resident. Irregularly abundant fall, winter, and spring visitor; generally distributed.
Varied Thrush	Casual winter and spring visitor; riparian and suburban areas.
Gray Catbird	Accidental. Oct. 7, 1975 {1}, Phoenix yard [BB]. Sept. 28, 1980 {1}. Slate Creek Divide [RW].
Northern Mockingbird	Common resident (abundant in suburban areas) in Lower and Upper Sonoran Zones. Absent from higher elevations in winter.
Sage Thrasher	Uncommon winter visitor, fairly common spring migrant; Upper Sonoran Zone, Lower Sonoran and saltbush deserts.
Brown Thrasher	Casual fall, winter, and spring visitor; riparian and suburban areas.
Bendire's Thrasher	Fairly common resident; Lower Sonoran Desert, hedgerows, farmyard edges, and mesquite trees.
Curve-billed Thrasher	Common resident; cholla deserts and suburban areas in Lower Sonoran Zones, and in some Upper Sonoran Zone habitats.
Crissal Thrasher	Uncommon local resident; riparian areas and washes in Lower Sonoran Zone; in chaparral at higher elevations.
Le Conte's Thrasher	Uncommon local resident; saltbush desert with tomatillo bushes and scattered shrubby mesquite trees.

Braces, {}, denote number of individuals, etc.   Brackets, [], denote observers or institutions

American Pipit – Yellow-throated Vireo

Species	Nest	Jan.	Feb.	Mar.	Apr.	May	June	July	Aug.	Sept.	Oct.	Nov.	Dec.
American Pipit													
Sprague's Pipit													
Bohemian Waxwing													
Cedar Waxwing	N												
Phainopepla	N												
Northern Shrike													
Loggerhead Shrike	N												
European Starling	N												
White-eyed Vireo													
Bell's Vireo	N												
Gray Vireo	N												
Solitary Vireo													
plumbeus form	N												
cassinii form													
Yellow-throated Vireo													

Legend:

Abundant	Common	Uncom. or Irreg.	Accidental
Irreg. Abund.	Fairly Com.	Rare or Casual	Ind. Extended Stay

- 106 -

American Pipit – Yellow-throated Vireo

American Pipit	Common transient and abundant winter visitor; fields, ponds, pastures, roadsides, and open riparian areas.
Sprague's Pipit	Rare winter visitor; fields, primarily those with alfalfa.
Bohemian Waxwing	Accidental. May 1, 1969 {1}, Seven Springs [ER,DTu].
Cedar Waxwing	Uncommon to abundant irregular fall, winter, and spring visitor; riparian and suburban areas.
Phainopepla	Common spring breeder, common fall and winter visitor, rare summer visitor; riparian areas and Lower Sonoran Desert, especially in trees with mistletoe.
Northern Shrike	Casual late fall and winter visitor to lowlands.
Loggerhead Shrike	Fairly common summer resident, common winter visitor; generally distributed.
European Starling	Abundant resident; Sonoran Zones.
White-eyed Vireo	Accidental. Nov. 16, 1975 {1}, n. w. Phoenix [DS]. Dec. 7, 1991 {1 found dead after being present for a week}, Phoenix Zoo [fide KI, TC]; specimen [UA]. May 27, 1992 {1}, e. of Mesa [MM].
Bell's Vireo	Common summer resident, one December record; riparian areas, especially in mesquite trees.
Gray Vireo	Fairly common summer resident; Upper Sonoran Zone, especially in juniper trees.
Solitary Vireo	
plumbeus form	Common summer resident in Transition Zone forests; fairly common transient and uncommon winter visitor in lowlands.
cassinii form	Fairly common transient and uncommon winter visitor in lowlards.
Yellow-throated Vireo	Casual vagrant; Lower and Upper Sonoran Zones.

Braces, { }, denote number of individuals, etc.   Brackets, [ ], denote observers or institutions

Hutton's Vireo – Yellow Warbler

Species	Nest	Jan.	Feb.	Mar.	Apr.	May	June	July	Aug.	Sept.	Oct.	Nov.	Dec.
Hutton's Vireo	N												
Warbling Vireo			·	····				·	━━━	━━━	····		·
Philadelphia Vireo										·	···		
Red-eyed Vireo						··		·		····	·		·
Yellow-green Vireo								~~~~				~	
Blue-winged Warbler							·						
Golden-winged Warbler				·	·				·				··
Tennessee Warbler						·····				····	···	·	
Orange-crowned Warbler		┃	·	·	·	━━			┃	┃	┃	┃	┃
Nashville Warbler		·	·	·	----	----			┃	┃	·	·	···
Virginia's Warbler	N			----	----				┃	┃	·	·	·
Lucy's Warbler	N		·	━━	━━			·	━━━	━━	·	·	·
Northern Parula		·····	··	··	··	·	~	·	·	·	·	····	·
Yellow Warbler	N	·····		━━━	━━	━━			████	███	━━━	····	████

Legend

████ Abundant	━━━ Common	------ Uncom. or Irreg.
▪▪▪▪ Irreg. Abund.	── Fairly Com.	········ Rare or Casual
		· Accidental
		~~ Ind. Extended Stay

Hutton's Vireo – Yellow Warbler

Hutton's Vireo Uncommon resident in Transition Zone oaks. Uncommon transient and winter visitor at lower elevations, especially in riparian areas. Rare breeder at lower elevations.

Warbling Vireo Common transient, three winter records; Lower and Upper Sonoran Zones.

Philadelphia Vireo Casual fall vagrant; Lower Sonoran Zone.

Red-eyed Vireo Rare transient; riparian and suburban areas in lowlands.

Yellow-green Vireo Accidental. July 13, 1980 {1}, Paloma [GR *et al.*, photo RW].

Blue-winged Warbler Accidental. June 14, 1991 {♂}, Coon Bluff [SD].

Golden-winged Warbler Accidental. Nov. 12–19, 1994 {♂}, Paloma [DK, TC *et al.*, photo R Jo].

Tennessee Warbler Rare transient, casual early winter visitor; riparian and suburban areas in lowlands.

Orange-crowned Warbler Common transient and winter visitor; riparian and suburban areas in lowlands.

Nashville Warbler Fairly common fall transient, uncommon spring transient, casual winter visitor; riparian and suburban areas in lowlands.

Virginia's Warbler Fairly common summer resident in oak and pine forests in Transition Zone. Uncommon transient in lowlands.

Lucy's Warbler Common summer resident, two December records; riparian areas, Lower and Upper Sonoran Zones, especially in mesquite trees.

Northern Parula Casual transient and winter visitor; riparian and suburban areas in lowlands.

Yellow Warbler Common summer resident, abundant fall transient, rare winter visitor; riparian and suburban areas in lowlands.

Braces, {}, denote number of individuals, etc.   Brackets, [], denote observers or institutions

Chestnut-sided Warbler – Grace's Warbler

Species	Nest	Jan.	Feb.	Mar.	Apr.	May	June	July	Aug.	Sept.	Oct.	Nov.	Dec.
Chestnut-sided Warbler													
Magnolia Warbler													
Cape May Warbler													
Black-throated Blue Warbler													
Yellow-rumped Warbler													
"Audubon's"													
"Myrtle"													
Black-throated Gray Warbler	N												
Townsend's Warbler													
Hermit Warbler													
Black-throated Green Warbler													
Blackburnian Warbler													
Yellow-throated Warbler													
Grace's Warbler	N												

Legend:

▮ Abundant	Common	Uncom. or Irreg.	· Accidental
▬ Irreg. Abund.	Fairly Com.	Rare or Casual	~~~ Ind. Extended Stay

Chestnut-sided Warbler – Grace's Warbler

Chestnut-sided Warbler	Rare transient and rare to uncommon winter visitor in small numbers; riparian and suburban areas in lowlands.
Magnolia Warbler	Casual fall transient; riparian and suburban areas.
Cape May Warbler	Accidental. Oct. 30, 1976 {1}, Sycamore Creek, Sunflower [ST, JW]. Dec. 22–24, 1986 {1}, Fountain Hills [AC, MBd, RB et al.].
Black-throated Blue Warbler	Casual fall transient; riparian areas.
Yellow-rumped Warbler	
"Audubon's"	Abundant transient and winter visitor; riparian and suburban areas.
"Myrtle"	Uncommon transient and winter visitor; riparian and suburban areas.
Black-throated Gray Warbler	Common summer resident in pinyon/juniper and oak woodlands. Fairly common transient and rare to uncommon winter visitor in lowland riparian and suburban areas.
Townsend's Warbler	Fairly common transient and irregular winter visitor in lowland riparian and suburban areas. Sometimes common transient at higher elevations, especially in fall.
Hermit Warbler	Uncommon transient and casual early winter visitor in lowland riparian and suburban areas. Uncommon to fairly common transient in Transition Zone forests.
Black-throated Green Warbler	Casual transient in lowland riparian and suburban areas.
Blackburnian Warbler	Accidental. Sept. 28, 1975 {1}, Tempe yard [ST]. Sept. 23, 1978 {1}, Chandler Blvd.[KK, JW].
Yellow-throated Warbler	Accidental. Apr. 14, 1979 {1}, Verde River [KR et al.]. Sept. 29 – Oct. 6, 1991 {1}, Granite Reef Picnic Area [SG, TC, LH et al.].
Grace's Warbler	Fairly common transient and summer resident in Transition Zone forests.

Braces, {}, denote number of individuals, etc.   Brackets, [ ], denote observers or institutions

Pine Warbler – Common Yellowthroat

Species	Nest	Jan.	Feb.	Mar.	Apr.	May	June	July	Aug.	Sept.	Oct.	Nov.	Dec.
Pine Warbler		~~~	~~~	~									~
Palm Warbler		···	···								···	···	···
Bay-breasted Warbler					·					·	·	·	
Blackpoll Warbler								~			·	~	
Black-and-white Warbler		---		·		:	:		·	---	:	~	
American Redstart		---		·	··	·	:	·					
Prothonotary Warbler											·		·
Worm-eating Warbler		~~~~	~~~~	~~~			·				·		~~~
Ovenbird		···	···			··	·						··
Northern Waterthrush		·		·	---	---			---	···			···
Louisiana Waterthrush		~		---	---								
Kentucky Warbler										·		~	
Macgillivray's Warbler		·				---					···		
Common Yellowthroat	N	---		---	---	■■■	■■■		■■■					

Legend:

Abundant (━━━)	Common (——)	Uncom. or Irreg. (------)
Irreg. Abund. (▪▪▪)	Fairly Com. (—)	Rare or Casual (·······)
	Accidental (•)	
	Ind. Extended Stay (~~~~)	

Pine Warbler – Common Yellowthroat

Pine Warbler Accidental. Dec. 10, 1990 – Mar. 4, 1991 {1}, Mesa yard [SH, MH *et al*, photo RW].

Palm Warbler Casual fall transient and winter visitor; riparian and suburban areas.

Bay-breasted Warbler Casual transient; riparian and suburban areas.

Blackpoll Warbler Casual fall transient; riparian and suburban areas.

Black-and-white Warbler Uncommon transient and winter visitor, two summer records; riparian and suburban areas.

American Redstart Uncommon transient and winter visitor, rare summer visitor; riparian and suburban areas.

Prothonotary Warbler Accidental. Dec. 27, 1977 {♀}, confluence of Salt and Gila Rivers; specimen [REA]. Oct. 26, 1987 {♂}, Phoenix yard [SD *et al*, photo RW].

Worm-eating Warbler Accidental. Oct. 17, 1957 {1}, n.w. Phoenix [SD *et al*]. Jan. 19, 1983 {1}, Verde River [ML]. Nov. 22, 1988 through Mar. 18, 1989 {1} Tempe yard [KG].

Ovenbird Rare transient and casual winter visitor; riparian and suburban areas.

Northern Waterthrush Uncommon transient and rare early winter visitor; riparian and suburban areas.

Louisiana Waterthrush Accidental. Jan. 21-31, 1987 {1}, Seven Springs [HB, SD *et al*].

Kentucky Warbler Accidental. Nov. 3-5, 1977 {1}, Salt River, s.w. Phoenix [GR *et al*].

MacGillivray's Warbler Fairly common transient, casual early winter visitor; riparian and suburban areas.

Common Yellowthroat Common local summer resident, fairly common winter visitor in reed and tall grass marshes. Uncommon transient; marshes and suburban areas.

Braces, { }, denote number of individuals, etc.   Brackets, [ ], denote observers or institutions

Hooded Warbler – Pyrrhuloxia

Species	Nest	Jan.	Feb.	Mar.	Apr.	May	June	July	Aug.	Sept.	Oct.	Nov.	Dec.
Hooded Warbler													
Wilson's Warbler													
Canada Warbler													
Red-faced Warbler													
Painted Redstart	N												
Yellow-breasted Chat	N												
Olive Warbler	N												
Hepatic Tanager	N												
Summer Tanager	N												
Scarlet Tanager													
Western Tanager	N												
Northern Cardinal	N												
Pyrrhuloxia	N												

Legend:

- • Accidental
- ~~~ Ind. Extended Stay
- ----- Uncom. or Irreg.
- .... Rare or Casual
- —— Common
- — Fairly Com.
- ▬ Abundant
- ▪▪▪▪▪ Irreg. Abund.

- 114 -

Hooded Warbler – Pyrrhuloxia

Hooded Warbler Casual visitor; suburban and riparian areas in lowlands.

Wilson's Warbler Common transient (sometimes abundant in fall); riparian and suburban areas in Sonoran and Transition Zones. Rare, irregular winter visitor in lowlands.

Canada Warbler Accidental. Sept. 23–24, 1981 {1}, Tempe [AL *et al.*]. Sept. 8, 1992 {1}, Chandler Blvd.[CB *et al.*].

Red-faced Warbler Uncommon transient in Transition Zone forests. Casual transient at lower elevations.

Painted Redstart Fairly common summer resident in Transition and high Upper Sonoran Zone forests. Rare transient and winter visitor in lowlands.

Yellow-breasted Chat Fairly common (locally common) summer resident; dense riparian areas in Sonoran Zones. Uncommon transient; suburban areas.

Olive Warbler Uncommon summer resident and rare winter resident in Transition Zone pines.

Hepatic Tanager Fairly common summer resident in Upper Sonoran and Transition Zone forests. Rare transient and casual winter visitor in lowlands.

Summer Tanager Common local summer resident; riparian areas. Rare late fall transient and casual winter visitor; riparian and suburban areas.

Scarlet Tanager Accidental. Nov. 27–28, 1979 {♀ or imm.}, Tempe [photo KR *et al.*]. Dec. 19, 1988 {♀}, Verde River [DS]. Nov. 4, 1994 {♂}, Phoenix [*fide* RB, photo CB].

Western Tanager Fairly common summer resident in Transition Zone forests. Common transient and casual winter visitor in lowlands.

Northern Cardinal Common resident; Lower and some Upper Sonoran Zone habitats.

Pyrrhuloxia Uncommon local resident; an influx of additional numbers in winter; dense brushy areas in Lower Sonoran Zone.

Braces, { }, denote number of individuals, etc.   Brackets, [ ], denote observers or institutions

Rose-breasted Grosbeak – Canyon Towhee

Species	Nest	Jan.	Feb.	Mar.	Apr.	May	June	July	Aug.	Sept.	Oct.	Nov.	Dec.
Rose-breasted Grosbeak													
Black-headed Grosbeak	N												
Blue Grosbeak	N												
Lazuli Bunting	N-1												
Indigo Bunting													
Varied Bunting	N												
Painted Bunting													
Dickcissel													
Green-tailed Towhee													
Spotted Towhee	N												
Canyon Towhee	N												

Legend:

▬ Abundant	─ Common
▪▪▪ Irreg. Abund.	─ Fairly Com.
------- Uncom. or Irreg.	• Accidental
••••••• Rare or Casual	~~~ Ind. Extended Stay

Rose-breasted Grosbeak – Canyon Towhee

Rose-breasted Grosbeak Rare transient and casual winter visitor; Lower Sonoran Zone and suburban areas.

Black-headed Grosbeak Fairly common summer resident in Transition Zone forests. Common transient in Sonoran Zones. Casual winter visitor in lowlands.

Blue Grosbeak Fairly common local summer resident, two December records; riparian areas in Sonoran Zones.

Lazuli Bunting Common transient, casual winter visitor, one summer record; Sonoran Zones: weedy and shrubby areas along irrigation ditches and other bodies of water, and suburban areas. One nesting record: May 27, 1976 {♀ on nest} Lower Camp Creek [ST].

Indigo Bunting Rare transient and summer visitor; riparian areas and pecan groves.

Varied Bunting Rare local resident in Sauceda Mts. and Sand Tank Mts., s.e. of Gila Bend [DG, PH].

Painted Bunting Accidental. Sept. 6, 1994 {imm.}, Chandler Blvd. [R Jo, SG]. Sept. 19–21, 1994 {imm.}, Granite Reef Picnic Area [JBu, SG].

Dickcissel Casual fall transient; weedy areas in lowlands.

Green-tailed Towhee Fairly common transient and winter visitor; Sonoran Zones: brushy areas, riparian and suburban areas.

Spotted Towhee Fairly common resident; brushy areas, especially chaparral, in Upper Sonoran and Transition Zones. Uncommon transient and uncommon irregular winter visitor; brushy areas, riparian and suburban areas at lower elevations. Some Transition Zone birds may move down slope in winter.

Canyon Towhee Common local resident; upper elevations of Lower Sonoran desert scrub and Upper Sonoran chaparral.

Braces, { }, denote number of individuals, etc.   Brackets, [ ], denote observers or institutions

– 117 –

Abert's Towhee – Black-throated Sparrow

Species	Nest	Jan.	Feb.	Mar.	Apr.	May	June	July	Aug.	Sept.	Oct.	Nov.	Dec.
Abert's Towhee	N												
Cassin's Sparrow													
Rufous-winged Sparrow													
Rufous-crowned Sparrow	N												
Chipping Sparrow													
Clay-colored Sparrow													
Brewer's Sparrow													
Black-chinned Sparrow	N												
Vesper Sparrow													
Lark Sparrow													
Black-throated Sparrow	N												

Legend:

Abundant | Common | Uncom. or Irreg. | Accidental

Irreg. Abund. | Fairly Com. | Rare or Casual | Ind. Extended Stay

Abert's Towhee – Black-throated Sparrow

Species	Description
Abert's Towhee	Abundant resident in riparian areas, locally common resident in suburban areas; Lower Sonoran Zone.
Cassin's Sparrow	Casual and irregular visitor following exceptional rainy periods in late summer; two spring records, one December record; weedy areas in Lower Sonoran Zone.
Rufous-winged Sparrow	Apr. 13, 1995 {2 singing males}, Sand Tank Mts., s.e. of Gila Bend [DG, PH]. Probably an uncommon summer resident in these mountains which were birded for the first time only recently.
Rufous-crowned Sparrow	Fairly common local resident; open grassy and rocky hillsides in Upper Sonoran Zone. Irregularly, a few individuals may descend to lower elevations in winter.
Chipping Sparrow	Common fall transient, fairly common winter visitor and spring transient; brushy areas and riparian edges in Lower and Upper Sonoran and Transition Zones.
Clay-colored Sparrow	Accidental. Nov. 27, 1975 {1}, Tempe [ST]. Apr. 29, 1977 {1}, Tempe [ST]. Nov. 7, 1979 {1}, Guernsey Ranch, s.w. Phoenix [ST, GR].
Brewer's Sparrow	Abundant transient; Lower and Upper Sonoran Zone deserts, field edges, and suburban areas. Common winter visitor; Lower Sonoran Zone desert and field edges.
Black-chinned Sparrow	Fairly common local summer resident; Upper Sonoran Zone chaparral and open pinyon/juniper. Rare local transient and winter visitor; rocky hillsides in Lower Sonoran Zone. Three lowland records.
Vesper Sparrow	Fairly common transient and winter visitor; open weedy fields, roadsides, and grassy areas in Sonoran Zones.
Lark Sparrow	Common transient, fairly common winter visitor; brushy, weedy areas, riparian areas, and field edges in Sonoran Zones.
Black-throated Sparrow	Common local resident; desert scrub in Sonoran Zones.

Braces, { }, denote number of individuals, etc.   Brackets, [ ], denote observers or institutions

Sage Sparrow – Harris' Sparrow

Species	Nest	Jan.	Feb.	Mar.	Apr.	May	June	July	Aug.	Sept.	Oct.	Nov.	Dec.
Sage Sparrow													
Lark Bunting													
Savannah Sparrow													
Grasshopper Sparrow													
Fox Sparrow													
Song Sparrow	N												
Lincoln's Sparrow													
Swamp Sparrow													
White-throated Sparrow													
Golden-crowned Sparrow													
White-crowned Sparrow													
Harris' Sparrow													

Legend:

Abundant	Common	Uncom. or Irreg.	• Accidental
Irreg. Abund.	Fairly Com.	Rare or Casual	~~~ Ind. Extended Stay

Sage Sparrow – Harris' Sparrow

Sage Sparrow	Fairly common local winter visitor; open saltbush and inkweed desert.
Lark Bunting	Common transient and (irregularly abundant) winter visitor; brushy desert and field edges in Lower Sonoran Zone.
Savannah Sparrow	Fairly common transient and fairly common to locally abundant winter visitor; open fields, roadsides, and grassy areas in Lower Sonoran Zone.
Grasshopper Sparrow	Casual fall and early winter transient; only four records, two of which were in atypical habitats of marsh and desert respectively.
Fox Sparrow	Rare, irregular winter visitor; dense, brushy and riparian areas in Sonoran Zones.
Song Sparrow	Common resident; numbers augmented by winter visitors from farther north; riparian areas, marshes, and vegetated lakesides in Sonoran Zones.
Lincoln's Sparrow	Fairly common (sometimes common) transient and winter visitor; riparian areas, marshes, brushy fields, and hedgerows in Sonoran Zones.
Swamp Sparrow	Rare to uncommon winter visitor; marshy areas, especially those with cattails and bulrushes, in Lower Sonoran Zone.
White-throated Sparrow	Uncommon transient and winter visitor; riparian and suburban areas in Lower Sonoran Zone.
Golden-crowned Sparrow	Rare winter visitor; riparian and other brushy areas in Lower Sonoran Zone. Sometimes with flocks of White-crowned Sparrows.
White-crowned Sparrow	Abundant transient and winter visitor, often in flocks; suburban, riparian, and other brushy areas in Sonoran Zones.
Harris' Sparrow	Rare winter visitor; more common during infrequent invasion years; suburban, riparian, and other brushy areas in Sonoran Zones. Sometimes with flocks of White-crowned Sparrows.

Braces, {}, denote number of individuals, etc.   Brackets, [], denote observers or institutions

Dark-eyed Junco– Brewer's Blackbird

Species	Nest	Jan.	Feb.	Mar.	Apr.	May	June	July	Aug.	Sept.	Oct.	Nov.	Dec.
Dark-eyed Junco													
"Oregon"													
"Gray-headed"													
"Slate-colored"													
Yellow-eyed Junco													
Mccown's Longspur													
Lapland Longspur													
Chestnut-collared Longspur													
Bobolink													
Red-winged Blackbird	N												
Eastern Meadowlark													
Western Meadowlark	N												
Yellow-headed Blackbird	N												
Rusty Blackbird													
Brewer's Blackbird													

Legend:

Abundant	Common	Uncom. or Irreg.
Irreg. Abund.	Fairly Com.	Rare or Casual
Accidental		
Ind. Extended Stay		

- 122 -

Dark-eyed Junco – Brewer's Blackbird

Dark-eyed Junco
"Oregon" Common winter visitor to lowlands.
"Gray-headed" Fairly common winter visitor to lowlands.
"Slate-colored" Rare winter visitor to lowlands.

Yellow-eyed Junco Accidental. Jan. 13, 1971 {1}, Seven Springs [SD, ER]. Oct. 27–28, 1974 {2}, Superstition Mts. [RN, JW *et al.*].

McCown's Longspur Accidental. Feb. 6–25, 1979 {♂}, with Chestnut-collareds in fallow field, s.w. Phoenix [ST, photo KR, m.ob.].

Lapland Longspur Accidental. Dec. 17–18, 1976 {1}, alfalfa field, s.w. Phoenix [KK *et al.*].

Chestnut-collared Longspur Uncommon transient and winter visitor; open grassy fields in Lower Sonoran Zone.

Bobolink Casual transient; weedy areas.

Red-winged Blackbird Common summer resident, abundant winter visitor; riparian areas, irrigated fields, marshes, and feedlots.

Eastern Meadowlark Uncommon winter visitor; fields in Lower Sonoran Zone. Usually found in more dense cover than Western Meadowlark.

Western Meadowlark Fairly common summer resident, common winter visitor; fields and other open areas, including deserts, in Sonoran Zones.

Yellow-headed Blackbird Uncommon local summer resident in marshes along Salt and Gila Rivers. Common winter visitor (sometimes locally abundant); marshes, fields, and feedlots.

Rusty Blackbird Casual winter visitor in wet areas.

Brewer's Blackbird Abundant winter visitor; fields, farmyards, feedlots, ponds, and riparian areas.

Braces, { }, denote number of individuals, etc.   Brackets, [ ], denote observers or institutions

Great-tailed Grackle – Cassin's Finch

Species	Nest	Jan.	Feb.	Mar.	Apr.	May	June	July	Aug.	Sept.	Oct.	Nov.	Dec.
Great-tailed Grackle	N	▇	▇	▇	▇	▇	▇	▇	▇	▇	▇	▇	▇
Common Grackle		~~~											~
Bronzed Cowbird	N	----	----	----	----	----	----	----	----	----	----	----	----
Brown-headed Cowbird	N	▇	▇	▇	▇	▇	▇	▇	▇	▇	▇	▇	▇
Orchard Oriole		····					··				····		
Hooded Oriole	N	····			▇	│	│	│	│	▇	│	····	····
Streak-backed Oriole						~~~	~~~						
Baltimore Oriole									·	·		·	
Bullock's Oriole	N		·	----					----	│	│	·	···
Scott's Oriole	N	·										·	·
Pine Grosbeak											~~~		
Purple Finch		····			····					····			
Cassin's Finch		----				----					----		

	Abundant ▇	Common ▇	Uncom. or Irreg. ------	Accidental ·
	Irreg. Abund. ▪▪▪	Fairly Com. ──	Rare or Casual ····	Ind. Extended Stay ~~~

Great-tailed Grackle – Cassin's Finch

Great-tailed Grackle	Common resident; riparian areas, ponds, marshes, farmyards, and suburban areas.
Common Grackle	Accidental. Dec. 18, 1984 – Jan. 23, 1985 {1}, Lake Pleasant [TC, photo GR]. Dec. 21, 1987 {1}, Salt River Indian Reservation [TH].
Bronzed Cowbird	Fairly common local summer resident; riparian and suburban areas. Uncommon local winter resident; feedlots and Phoenix Zoo.
Brown-headed Cowbird	Common resident; generally distributed. In winter, flocks found with other blackbirds in feedlots and fields, sometimes abundantly.
Orchard Oriole	Casual transient and winter visitor in lowlands.
Hooded Oriole	Common summer resident, casual winter visitor; riparian and suburban areas (often nesting in palm trees) in Sonoran Zones.
Streak-backed Oriole	Accidental. Apr. 4, 1976 {♂}, confluence of Salt and Gila Rivers [ST, SB].
Baltimore Oriole	Casual visitor. One nesting record with Bullock's Oriole: June 1980, Verde River [KR *et al.*].
Bullock's Oriole	Fairly common local summer resident, casual winter visitor; riparian areas in Sonoran Zones. Fairly common transient throughout Sonoran and Transition Zones.
Scott's Oriole	Uncommon local summer resident in upper Lower Sonoran and Upper Sonoran Zones: *Yucca elata*, chaparral, evergreen oak, and pinyon/juniper habitats. Rare transient in Lower Sonoran Zone riparian and suburban areas. One December record.
Pine Grosbeak	Accidental. Mid-Oct. – early Nov., 1972 {♂, freshly dead}, Gila Bend Air Base [*fide* RJ].
Purple Finch	Rare transient and winter visitor; riparian and suburban areas, and lower slopes of Mazatzal Mts.
Cassin's Finch	Irregular transient and winter visitor; Sonoran and Transition Zones.

Braces, { }, denote number of individuals, etc.	Brackets, [ ], denote observers or institutions

House Finch – House Sparrow

Species	Nest	Jan.	Feb.	Mar.	Apr.	May	June	July	Aug.	Sept.	Oct.	Nov.	Dec.
House Finch	N												
Red Crossbill	N-1												
Pine Siskin													
Lesser Goldfinch	N												
Lawrence's Goldfinch	N-3												
American Goldfinch													
Evening Grosbeak													
House Sparrow	N												

Legend:

Abundant	Accidental
Irreg. Abund.	Ind. Extended Stay
Common	Uncom. or Irreg.
Fairly Com.	Rare or Casual

House Finch – House Sparrow

House Finch	Abundant resident; riparian and suburban areas, farmlands, and desert in Sonoran Zones.
Red Crossbill	Irregular visitor; riparian and suburban areas, especially in pines, in Sonoran and Transition Zones. One nesting record: Mar. 26, 1976 {adult pair with young} Encanto Park [KK, JW].
Pine Siskin	Irregular winter visitor to lowlands. Rare summer visitor to Transition Zone forests.
Lesser Goldfinch	Fairly common summer resident; riparian areas. Common winter visitor; riparian and weedy areas. Sonoran Zones.
Lawrence's Goldfinch	Irregular winter visitor; weedy fields and riparian areas. Three nesting records: Apr. 10, 1977 {pair with young} Verde River [ST, AG], May 7, 1978 {two pairs on nests} Verde River [KK, GR], and late June 1980 {juveniles} Hassayampa River [*fide* CT].
American Goldfinch	Uncommon winter visitor; weedy and riparian areas.
Evening Grosbeak	Rare irregular visitor; Sonoran and Transition Zones.
House Sparrow	Abundant resident wherever humans live.

Braces, { }, denote number of individuals, etc.   Brackets, [ ], denote observers or institutions

ADDENDUM

ADDITIONAL SPECIES

Mew Gull: Jan. 9 – Feb. 6, 1996 {1 first winter}, Painted Rock Dam [DS *et al.,* photo RW].

Thayer's Gull: Jan. 11 – Feb. 15, 1996 {1 first winter}, Painted Rock Dam [SB *et al.,* photo RW].

Hudsonian Godwit: May 18, 1996 {1}, Gila Bend Sewage Ponds [photo CB *et al.*].

HYPOTHETICAL

Buff-breasted Sandpiper: Sept. 26, 1993 {1}, Painted Rock Dam [DS *et al.*]. Undocumented by photo. No previous state records.

ADDITIONAL BIRDING AREA

Kiwanis Park, Tempe

The lake at this park is worth checking for unusual water birds. Neotropic Cormorant, White-winged Scoter, and Heermann's Gull are some of the unusual birds that have occurred here. The park is located on the south side of Baseline Road, 0.7 of a mile west of Rural Road. (See County Map, inside back cover, for location of Baseline and Rural Roads).

SUGGESTED READING

Additional aids to birding in Maricopa County and Arizona can be found in the following publications.

LOCAL PUBLICATION

The Cactus Wrendition (formerly *The Roadrunner*). Published bimonthly by the Maricopa Audubon Society. Contains notices of meetings, field trips, and field observations.

FIELD GUIDES

Clark, William S., and Brian K. Wheeler. 1987. *A Field Guide to Hawks of North America*. Houghton Mifflin, Boston.

Dunne, Pete, David Sibley, and Clay Sutton. 1988. *Hawks In Flight*. Houghton Mifflin, Boston.

Hayman, Peter, John Marchant, and Tony Prater. 1986. *Shorebirds: An Identification Guide to the Waders of the World*. Houghton Mifflin, Boston.

Howell, Steve N. G., and Sophie Webb. 1995. *A Guide to the Birds of Mexico and Northern Central America*. Oxford University Press, New York.

Kaufman, Kenn. 1990. *A Field Guide to Advanced Birding*. Houghton Mifflin, Boston.

Peterson, Roger T. 1990. *A Field Guide to Western Birds*. Third Edition. Houghton Mifflin, Boston.

_____, and Edward L. Chalif. 1973. *A Field Guide to Mexican Birds*. Houghton Mifflin, Boston.

Scott, Shirley L. (ed.). 1987. *Field Guide to the Birds of North America*. Second Edition. National Geographic Society, Washington D. C.

Zimmer, Kevin J. 1985. *The Western Birdwatcher*. Prentice Hall, Inc., New Jersey. Contains field identificaton aids for species in Arizona and other western states.

JOURNALS AND MAGAZINES

Birder's World, published bimonthy by Kalmbach Publishing Co. Contains field identification articles.

Birding, published bimonthly by the American Birding Association. Contains field identification articles.

Continental Birdlife, published 1979-1981 by Kenn Kaufman and Janet Witzeman. Contains field identification articles.

Field Notes (formerly *American Birds*), published five times a year by the National Audubon Society, New York. Contains seasonal coverage of bird occurrence and distribution in Arizona as well as other regions in the U.S. and Canada; plus (in *American Birds*) field identification articles.

Western Birds (formerly *California Birds*), published quarterly by Western Field Ornithologists. Contains some field identification articles, plus articles of unusual records in Arizona and other western states.

FIELD IDENTIFICATION ARTICLES

Clark, William S. 1981. Flight Identification of Common North American Buteos. *Continental Birdlife* 2: 129-143.

_____. 1984. Field Identification of Accipiters in North America. *Birding* 16: 251-263.

Dunn, Jon L. 1978. The Races of Yellow-bellied Sapsuckers. *Birding* 10: 142-149 (reprinted from *Western Tanager* 44, No. 7).

_____, and Kimball L. Garrett. 1990. The Identification of Ruddy and Common Ground-Doves. *Birding* 22: 138-145.

Kaufman, Kenn. 1979. Identifying "Myrtle" and "Audubon's" Warblers Out of Breeding Plumage. *Continental Birdlife* 1: 89-92.

_____. 1983. Identifying Streak-backed Orioles: A Note of Caution. *American Birds* 37: 140-141.

_____. 1986. ID Counterpoint: More On Accipters. *Birding* 18: 208-209.

Kaufman, Kenn. 1994. Savannah Sparrows. *Birder's World* 8 (6): 76-77.

Kaufman, Kenn. 1986-1994. The Practiced Eye:

Identifying Monochrome Grebes in Winter. *American Birds* 46: 1187-1190.

Summertime Blues (Little Blue Heron, Snowy Egret, and white-morph Reddish Egret). *American Birds* 45: 330-333.

Immature Night-Herons. *American Birds* 42: 169-171.

Female Dabbling Ducks. *American Birds* 42: 1203-1205.

Common Merganser and Red-breasted Merganser. *American Birds* 44: 1203-1205.

Buteos of the Winter Fields. *American Birds* 43: 1241-1244.

Pectoral Sandpiper and Sharp-tailed Sandpiper. *American Birds* 41: 1356-1358.

Curlew Sandpiper and its I.D. Contenders. *American Birds* 44: 189-192.

Terns Overhead. *American Birds* 41: 184-187.

Comparing the Screech-Owls. *American Birds* 43: 203-206.

Lucifer Hummingbird Identification. *American Birds* 46: 491-494.

Red-naped Sapsucker and Yellow-bellied Sapsucker. *American Birds* 42: 348-350.

Identifying the Hairy Woodpecker (compared with Downy and Three-toed Woodpeckers). *American Birds* 47: 311-314.

A Flicker of Recognition: Three Distinct Forms and Their Off-spring. *American Birds* 45: 1172-1175.

Western Kingbird Identification (compared with Tropical and Cassin's Kingbirds). *American Birds* 46: 323-326.

Scrub Jay and Gray-breasted Jay. *American Birds* 44: 5-6.

Kaufman, Kenn. 1986-1994. The Practiced Eye (Cont.):

Bluebirds. *American Birds* 46: 159-162.

Curve-billed Thrasher and Bendire's Thrasher. *American Birds* 44: 359-362.

Identifying Hutton's Vireo. *American Birds* 47: 460-462.

Yellow Warbler and its I.D. Contenders. *American Birds* 45: 167-170.

Notes on Female Tanagers. *American Birds* 42: 3-5.

Blue Grosbeak and Indigo Bunting. *American Birds* 43: 385-388.

Notes on Female Orioles. *American Birds* 41: 3-4.

Cassin's Finch Versus Purple Finch. *American Birds* 40: 1124-1127.

Notes on Goldfinch Identification. *American Birds* 47: 159-162.

Changes in Latitude, Changes in Plumage. *American Birds* 48: 29-32.

Kaufman, Kenn. 1995. Black-bellied Plover (compared with American Golden-Plover). *Birder's World* 9 (4): 68-69.

Landing, James E. 1991. On Yellow-bellied Sapsuckers with Red Napes. *Birding* 23: 20-22.

Lehman, Paul. 1991. Notes on Plumage Variation in Adult Red-naped and Red-breasted Sapsuckers. *Birding* 23: 23-26.

Rosenberg, Gary H. 1990. Arizona Birding Pitfalls.

Part I: Species We Take For Granted. *Birding* 22: 120-129. Includes problems in identifying Bendire's and Curve-billed Thrashers, Clay-colored, Chipping, and Brewer's Sparrows, and Cassin's Finch, as well as sapsuckers, ravens, vireos, and meadowlarks.

Part II: The Mexican Connection. *Birding* 22: 176-184. Discusses strays from Mexico and status of Aplomado Falcon.

Simon, David. 1977. Identification of Clay-colored, Brewer's, and Chipping Sparrows in Fall Plumage. *Birding* 9: 189-191.

Terrill, Scott B., and Linda S. Terrill. 1981. On the Field Identification of Yellow-green, Red-eyed, Philadelphia, and Warbling Vireos. *Continental Birdlife* 2: 144-149.

Veit, Richard R., and Lars Jonsson. 1984. Field Identification of Smaller Sandpipers Within the Genus *Calidris*. *American Birds* 38: 853-876 (reprinted 41: 212-236).

Whitney, Bret, and Kenn Kaufman. 1985-1987. The *Empidonax* Challenge.

> Part I: Introduction. *Birding* 17: 151-158.
>
> Part II: Least, Hammond's, and Dusky Flycatchers. *Birding* 17: 277-287.
>
> Part III: Willow and Alder Flycatchers. *Birding* 18: 153-159.
>
> Part IV: Acadian, Yellow-bellied, and Western Flycatchers. *Birding* 18: 315-327.
>
> Part V: Buff-breasted and Gray Flycatchers. *Birding* 19: 7-15.

Wilds, Claudia. 1982. Separating the Yellowlegs. *Birding* 14: 172-178.

_____. 1993. Identification and Aging of Forster's and Common Terns. *Birding* 25: 94-108.

_____, and Mike Newlon. 1983. The Identification of Dowitchers. *Birding* 15: 151-165.

REGIONAL GUIDES

Babbitt, Charles. 1995. Birding the Kaibab Plateau, Arizona. *Winging It* (Newsletter of the American Birding Association) 7: (6) 1.

Brown, Bryan T., Steven W. Carothers, Lois T. Haight, R. Roy Johnson, and Meribeth M. Riffey. 1984. *Birds of the Grand Canyon Region*. Second Edition. Grand Canyon Natural History Association, Grand Canyon.

Glinski, Richard L. (ed.). In Press. *Raptors of Arizona.* University of Arizona Press, Tucson.

Jacobs, Brad. 1986. *Birding On the Navajo and Hopi Reservations.* Jacobs Publishing Co., Sycamore, Missouri.

LaRue, Charles T. 1994. *Birds of Northern Black Mesa, Navajo County, Arizona.* Reprinted from *The Great Basin Naturalist* 54: 1-63.

Monson, Gale, and Allan R. Phillips. 1981. *Annotated Checklist of the Birds of Arizona.* Second Edition. University of Arizona Press, Tucson.

Phillips, Allan R., Joe Marshall, and Gale Monson. 1964. *The Birds of Arizona.* University of Arizona Press, Tucson.

Rea, Amadeo M. 1983. *Once A River. Bird Life and Habitat Changes on the Middle Gila.* University of Arizona Press, Tucson.

Rosenberg, Gary H., and Scott B. Terrill. 1986. The Avifauna of Apache County, Arizona. *Western Birds* 17: 171-187.

_____, and Dave Stejskal (compilers). 1994. *The Arizona Bird Committee's Field Checklist of the Birds of Arizona.* The Arizona Bird Committee, Tucson.

Rosenberg, Kenneth V., Robert D. Ohmart, William C. Hunter, and Bertin W. Anderson. 1991. *Birds of the Lower Colorado River Valley.* University of Arizona Press, Tucson.

Russell, Stephen, and Gale Monson. In Press. *Birds of Sonora.* University of Arizona Press, Tucson.

Stejskal, David, and Gary Rosenberg. 1990. Birding the Lower Colorado River Valley (Parker to Lake Havasu). *Cactus Wrendition* 39: (1) 10.

Taylor, Richard C. 1995. *A Birder's Guide to Southeastern Arizona.* American Birding Association, Colorado Springs, Colorado.

Tucson Audubon Society (ed.). 1995. *Davis' and Russell's Finding Birds in Southeastern Arizona.* Fourth Edition. Tucson Audubon Society, Tucson.

RARE AND UNUSUAL BIRDS
DOCUMENTED IN MARICOPA COUNTY

Yellow-billed Loon at Painted Rock Dam, January 16, 1984. First state record. *Photo/Janet Witzeman.*

Brown Booby (immature) at Harbor Lakes, northwest Phoenix, September 20, 1990. First county record. *Photo/Tom Gatz.*

Magnificent Frigatebird (1 of 6 immatures) at Painted Rock Dam, July 22, 1979. *Photo/Janet Witzeman.*

Reddish Egret in Ahwatukee, July 15, 1980. First county record, fourth state record. *Photo/Robert Witzeman.*

White Ibis (part of a group of 10) on Verde River below Horseshoe Dam, May 11, 1977. First county record, second state record. *Photo/Dick Todd.*

Fulvous Whistling-Duck at Phoenix Zoo Ponds, October 26, 1993. *Photo/Jill Jones.*

Tufted Duck with Ring-necked Ducks at Red Mountain Ranch, Mesa, January 2, 1993. First state record. *Photo/Tom Gatz.*

Tufted Duck (same individual as above, showing tuft) at Red Mountain Ranch, Mesa, February 14, 1993. *Photo/Roy Jones.*

Black Scoters (3 females or immatures) at 35th Avenue Ponds, Phoenix, November 5, 1975. First state record. *Photo/Janet Witzeman.*

Surf Scoters (part of a group of 27) at the Chandler Ponds during a storm which also blew in 12 Greater Scaup, 8 Heermann's Gulls, 5 Herring Gulls, and 12 more Surf Scoters to Phoenix area ponds, November 28, 1975. *Photo/Robert Witzeman.*

Wandering Tattler at 35th Avenue Ponds, Phoenix, September 18, 1971. First state record. *Photo/Robert Witzeman.*

Ruff with Long-billed Dowitchers at 35th Avenue Ponds, Phoenix, November 15, 1974. First state record. *Photo/Janet Witzeman.*

Long-tailed Jaeger (juvenile) at 35th Avenue Ponds, Phoenix, September 7, 1970. First state record. *Photo/Robert Witzeman.*

Mew Gull (first winter) at Painted Rock Dam, January 11, 1996. First county record. *Photo/Robert Witzeman.*

Thayer's Gull (first winter) at Painted Rock Dam, January 11, 1996. First county record. *Photo/Robert Witzeman.*

Glaucous Gull (first winter) at Indian Bend Wash Park, Scottsdale, November 19, 1988. First state record. *Photo/Tom Gatz.*

Elegant Tern at Painted Rock Dam, May 30, 1988. First state record. *Photo/David Stejskal.*

Least Tern at Painted Rock Dam, July 10, 1974. First county record, fourth state record. *Photo/Robert Witzeman.*

Scissor-tailed Flycatcher in Gilbert, May 30, 1972. Third county record. *Photo/Lloyd Shuttleworth.*

Rufous-backed Robin in Carefree, November 15, 1966. First county record, third state record. *Photo/Eleanor Radke.*

Pine Warbler in Mesa, January 4, 1991. First county record, second state record. *Photo/Robert Witzeman.*

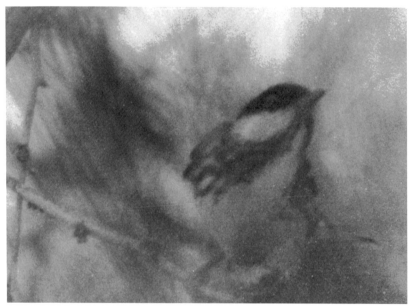

Blackpoll Warbler in northwest Phoenix, July 19, 1974. First county record, fourth state record. *Photo/Tom Stejskal.*

Prothonotary Warbler in northeast Phoenix, October 26, 1987. First county record. *Photo/Robert Witzeman.*

Scarlet Tanager (female or immature) in Tempe, November 27, 1979. First county record. *Photo/Kenneth V. Rosenberg.*

INDEX

**Powers Butte Wildlife
Area** 26,47,48
Pygmy-Owl
  Ferruginous.... 1,6,7,8,23, 88-89
  Northern.............................88-89
Pyrrhuloxia 8,53,114-115
Quail, Gambel's 78-79
Rackensack Gulch 37,38
Rail - See also Sora
  Clapper 8,20,78-79
  Virginia 8,21,78-79
Raven, Common 100-101
Redhead 70-71
Redstart
  American...................... 112-113
  Painted 37,114-115
Rio Verde 33,56
Roadrunner, Greater ... 2,29,33,34,
                          46,51,54,88-89
Robbins Butte Wildlife Area ... 47
Robin
  American.................... 5,104-105
  Rufous-backed............ 12,25,52,
                          104-105,144
Ruff 2,14,82-83,140
Saguaro Lake 35
Salt River 16,17,19,35,56
Sanderling 14,80-81
Sandpiper
  Baird's 82-83
  Buff-breasted 15,128
  Least 82-83
  Pectoral 82-83
  Semipalmated....................82-83
  Sharp-tailed 2,14,82-83
  Solitary 14,80-81
  Spotted 80-81
  Stilt 82-83
  Upland 80-81
  Western 82-83
Sapsucker
  Red-breasted 1,46,92-93
  Red-naped 1,39,46,52,92-93
  Williamson's 92-93
  Yellow-bellied 92-93

Scaup
  Greater.................. 19,31,72-73
  Lesser 72-73
Scoter
  Black 14,72-73,139
  Surf....................... 14,72-73,139
  White-winged ... 14,19,72-73,128
Scottsdale 29-31
Screech-Owl, Western ... 29,33,56,
                                    88-89
Scrub-Jay, Western.... 5,39,98-99
Seven Springs 37,38,39
Shoveler, Northern..............70-71
Shrike
  Loggerhead.............. 55,106-107
  Northern....................... 106-107
Siskin, Pine.................... 126-127
Skimmer, Black 15,86-87
Slate Creek Divide 36-37
Snipe, Common 29,82-83
Solitaire, Townsend's ..38,39,102-103
Sora 1,8,21,52,78-79
***South Mountain Park* -** See
  Phoenix South Mountain Park
Sparrow
  Black-chinned 36,37,38,39,
                                 118-119
  Black-throated .. 29,33,36,37,51,
                                 118-119
  Brewer's 118-119
  Cassin's........................ 118-119
  Chipping 118-119
  Clay-colored................. 118-119
  Fox 120-121
  Golden-crowned 58,120-121
  Grasshopper 120-121
  Harris'.................... 58,120-121
  House 126-127
  Lark 118-119
  Lincoln's 120-121
  Rufous-crowned 36,38,39,
                                 118-119
  Rufous-winged 118-119
  Sage 47,120-121
  Savannah 120-121

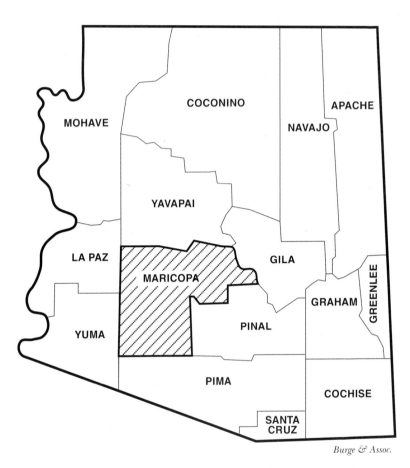

Burge & Assoc.

ARIZONA COUNTIES